Make a Windsor Chair

with

Michael Dunbar

Make a Windsor Chair
with
Michael Dunbar

Cover and text photos by Andrew Edgar

First printing: June 1984
International Standard Book Number: 0-918804-21-3
Library of Congress Catalog Card Number: 83-050681
Printed in the United States of America

A FINE WOODWORKING Book

FINE WOODWORKING® is a trademark of The Taunton Press, Inc.,
registered in the U.S. Patent and Trademark Office.

The Taunton Press, Inc.
52 Church Hill Road
Box 355
Newtown, Connecticut 06470

Acknowledgments

My approach to teaching Windsor chairmaking has been worked out in an unusual manner. I have spent the last several years traveling around the country teaching chairmaking in intensive, one-week courses. During that time, I met and worked with a number of people who helped me refine the methods I use to introduce Windsor chairmaking to novices. If you find this book helps you to make a chair and, even more important, to understand how the chair works, you are, as I am, in their debt. I give special thanks for their help and enthusiasm to Tom Hinckley, Ernie Conover, Jim Poropat, Tom Medhurst and Don Baldwin.

I would also like to thank Eddie Tremblay, who for years has been supplying me with all the logs that I need without ever complaining that I am too fussy about the quality of my firewood.

I would still be grateful to my wife, Carol, if she had merely tolerated my obsession. Instead, she has always encouraged and supported me. The recognition and success I have received belongs equally to her. This is my opportunity to inform my friends and readers of the important role she has played in my career, and it is my opportunity to thank her. I would, therefore, like to dedicate this book to her, to Duncan and to the Terrible Triplets.

Table of Contents

Introduction

I have been making Windsor chairs since 1970. When I started, I could find no books on how to make them, and no one who was making them to show me how. I learned by reading everything I could about Windsors, by examining old Windsors closely, and by trial and error in the workshop. I have written this book because it is the best way I could find to share what I have learned with a broad audience.

My fascination with Windsor chairs resulted from a happy accident. I was twenty-four years old, in college and recently married. I was working toward a degree in French, and my long-range plans called for eventually earning my doctorate. I had no experience working wood and, furthermore, had no interest in it whatsoever.

In order to save money, my wife, Carol, and I were furnishing our apartment with whatever we could cull from Goodwill and the Salvation Army. One spring morning we stopped at a yard sale. I wandered onto the porch, where I found myself looking at a small, black chair. It was so unusual that I could not ignore it; it seemed to insist that I look at it. Though the chair cost one quarter of our monthly rent, a sacrifice we could not make lightly, I could not bear to leave it behind.

In the following weeks, Carol would regularly awaken at night to find that I was not there. I had gotten up and gone to the parlor to stare at the chair. She must have feared for my sanity, for some nights she would find me studying the chair in a darkened room with a flashlight or by candlelight. I discovered a lot about this complex chair, including its marvelously subtle surface that changed character when viewed under these different light sources. I later found out that this surface was the result of the hand tools used by the craftsman to make the chair. I had never seen such a surface before because today's furniture surfaces are usually sanded to a boring, uniform texture.

At the public library, I discovered that my purchase was one of an almost unlimited variety of chairs known as Windsors. My fascination continued to grow so that by my senior year in college, I was in business part-time as a Windsor chairmaker. Before my graduation that year, I already had an order for fifty chairs. Since then, I have had no other career and have never desired one.

When introduced to North America in about 1750, Windsors were a revolutionary new concept in chair manufacture. From the time of the ancient Egyptians, chairs had been put together in one of two ways. Joined chairs were made by fitting square or rectangular tenons into similarly shaped mortises. Stick, or socketed, chairs had round tenons that were fitted into round sockets. Windsors are stick chairs, but prior to their introduction, the most familiar stick chair was the common ladder-back.

While joined chairs are time-consuming and expensive to make, round tenons and sockets can be made quickly—tenons by turning or whittling, sockets with a brace and bit. Stick chairs, therefore, have long been used for inexpensive, everyday seating. But most stick chairs are uncomfortable. Because the back is an extension of the rear legs, it cannot recline much before the balance of the chair is upset. A Windsor-chair back and legs are separate and both are anchored in a solid, wooden seat. The back can recline while the legs can be canted for stability. The development of Windsor chairs meant that at last a chair could be inexpensive and comfortable at the same time.

Making the back and undercarriage distinct and independent systems also allowed them to be interpreted in new ways. The craftsmen who were developing the Windsor form could approach the concept of a chair from a whole new point of view. The Windsor-chair designs that resulted from the craftsmen's explorations were so successful that they have become indelibly etched into the American collective consciousness. In this regard, Windsor chairs are perhaps one of the greatest success stories in the history of furniture design. Since the time they were introduced, American craftsmen have never stopped making them. The industrial revolution of the nineteenth century, which moved furniture production from the workshop to the factory, changed how Windsor chairs were made, but not their basic forms. In fact, the last new Windsor type was introduced about 1830. Every Windsor done since then has amounted to a reinterpretation of an existing style.

I have chosen a sack-back Windsor and a continuous-arm Windsor for this book because over the years they have proven, by far, to be the chairs that are most popular with my customers. These are not the only styles of Windsors, nor is every Windsor-chairmaking skill required in making them. But once you have mastered the skills needed for these two chairs, those needed for other Windsors can be inferred.

Both the sack-back and continuous-arm designs are derived from antique chairs I now own or have owned. The continuous arm was heavily influenced by a chair made in New York City about 1790, while the sack back is an amalgamation of several chairs of this style. (The model for my continuous arm is shown in Chapter XIII, along with other Windsors that I have made and antique chairs that I own.) My chairs, however, are not strict copies of the antiques. I have been making these chairs for a long time, and as my skill and perceptions grew, so my personal influence on the chairs increased. Over the years, the chairs have changed as I have changed. I am flattered if you find my taste worthy enough to copy. However, I know that as you become more experienced and competent as a chairmaker and as your insights into the Windsor-chair form grow, you will begin to impose your own personality on the designs. Just as my antique chairs reflect the personalities of their makers and my transformations of them reflect my personality, so will your copies of my chairs become your own distinct work.

Likewise, I have shown here how I make chairs, but my methods are not carved in stone (or in wood for that matter). Other chairmakers may do things in a different order, or may prefer different tools. I would not contest with them which methods are correct or better; I feel that success is the bottom line. If one method works as quickly and as well as another, it is equally valid.

Chair designs are personal, and the variations that are visually successful are infinite. The same can be said for the various techniques used in Windsor chairmaking. When it comes to the engineering of the chairs, however, I am not so tolerant. I definitely feel that some methods are superior to others. Those in this book are the ones that I have discovered to work the best and to be the most logical.

A week before writing this introduction, I taught a course in Windsor chairmaking in Los Angeles. As I showed how to assemble the parts, I described how they pushed or pulled against each other to compensate for the shortcomings of stick construction. One of my students, an aerospace engineer, exclaimed, "This is really high tech!" I was surprised, and remarked that the process was more than 200 years old. He explained that high tech does not necessarily mean modern, rather it describes any process at the cutting edge of human capability.

In that case, Windsors are high-tech chairs. This is evident not only in the chair's engineering, but in how the wood is selected and worked. Riving the parts from green wood allows them to be worked to dimensions that are much finer and more slender than is possible with kiln-dried wood, which is used for factory-made Windsors. The finished chair is much more delicate in its appearance than is a factory chair, which must have thicker parts to make up for the inferior quality of the wood. This delicacy will surprise a first-time viewer. A good handmade Windsor is delicate, but it is by no means fragile. In fact, the life span of such a chair is several times that of a human being. My observations of broken antique Windsors lead me to conclude that the damage is not generally due to failure of the construction, but rather failure of the wood, which has grown old and brittle and weak.

Writing this book was perhaps the most difficult thing I have ever done—it was far easier for me to teach myself to make Windsors than it has been to sit down and explain those skills on paper to someone else. In the following chapters, I am going to introduce you to an approach to wood and a way of working it that is probably markedly different from any of your other woodworking experiences. Here are some things to keep in mind as you read and work your way through the pages of the book.

Each Windsor chair, even if it is a member of a set, is slightly different. The length of a part or the position of a socket is often determined by the chair itself, not by a drawing. For example, the length of the stretchers must be calculated from the positions of the legs on the chair being made, not from a drawing or from a model chair. Over-reliance on drawings when making a Windsor is an invitation to trouble.

The measured drawings in Chapters XI and XII are based on two chairs that I use as models. My chairs all vary somewhat from these drawings, and yours will too. Refer to the measurements as a guide, but do not be a slave to them—the chair will tell you its own requirements.

I work with green wood split from a log. When I am chairmaking full-time, I use several logs a month. You will not be this voracious unless you, too, make chairs professionally. You should split parts from green logs to obtain the quality of the wood required to make Windsors, but do not worry about keeping the wood wet. Forget about such tricks as storing the wood in plastic bags or waxing the end grain. These can promote fungus attack and rot. If you cannot use up a log immediately, split out the wood suitable for chair parts as soon as possible and store it under shelter and off the ground. Split and stored like this, the log will keep indefinitely and can be used at any time, though when it is dry it will not work quite as easily as green wood.

When assembling your chair, do not use glue that sets up too quickly. I use and highly recommend a white, polyvinyl acetate glue, such as Elmer's Glue-All. Aliphatic resin, or yellow glue, such as Titebond, too often results in a tenon being twisted off the end of a stretcher when the stretchers are assembled because the glue seizes so quickly.

You will recognize many of the tools used in Windsor chairmaking, but you may not have encountered some of the others. I explain how to use each of these tools as they are introduced, and I discuss how to sharpen them in Chapter XIV. I found all my chairmaking tools at auctions, second-hand shops and through antique dealers. But a few of these tools had almost disappeared by the time I started hunting—it took me several years to find a full set of spoon bits, for example. A few years back, Ernie Conover, a friend of mine who is a tool maker, proposed reproducing several hard-to-find tools. He made patterns from my old scorp and spoon bits, and he is now offering reproductions of these tools through Conover Woodcraft Specialties, Inc., 18125 Madison Road, Parkman, Ohio, 44080.

A Windsor chair is assembled with parts that can be made separately. In fact, Windsor chairmakers often bought parts made by others, particularly turnings. I have begun the chairmaking in this book with the seat, because it is the physical and aesthetic center of the chair. When I am making chairs full-time, however, I organize the work so that I can produce two chairs in four days. To do this, I shape and bend the backs first thing on Monday, so that they will be dry and ready for assembly on Thursday. In chairmaking, as in any other business, time is money, and a chairmaker must be as efficient as he is skillful. As you gain experience, you will develop your own order of events to suit your own purposes. For your first chairs, however, I recommend that you follow the book—what you learn in one chapter will make the work in subsequent chapters easier to master.

Throughout the book, as each part is made, I also mention design considerations that make the part successful. Much of this design discussion is subjective; what one person considers good, another sees otherwise. I think, however, that it is possible for a chair to be made of nice-looking parts and still be a visual failure. A well-designed Windsor is subtle. It should not assault the viewer. Instead, when viewed in a room full of furniture, the eye should be delighted when it discovers a Windsor. To achieve this quality, I prefer to restrain each part, to make them robust but not exaggerated. A chair succeeds because of its unity, never because of just one feature. A subtle chair teases the viewer; the eye cannot notice everything at once. Therefore, each time you look at the chair, you will discover something about it.

I believe that it pays off to keep these thoughts on design in mind when in the shop. They will help you to make Windsors that not only are comfortable and durable, but good-looking, too. I cannot think of anything more that could be asked from a piece of furniture.

Chapter I

Sculpting the Seat

A Windsor chair begins with the seat. It is the one element common to all Windsor chairs, benches and stools. Windsor-chair backs vary in shape— some have bows, some have crests. The spindles of the backs also vary—some are turned to look like bamboo, others are whittled with more or less of a swelling. Some are even arrow-shaped. Legs can be baluster, double-bobbin or bamboo-shaped. Some stools have only three legs, and some settees have a dozen. The stretchers usually form an *H*-pattern or box pattern, but some form an *X,* or even a crescent with spurs. The solid-wood seat, into which the legs and back are socketed, is the one constant, and is what distinguishes Windsor chairs from all other types.

There are other reasons why a Windsor begins with the seat. Most of the other parts of a Windsor chair radiate from this point. The angles at which the leg sockets are bored into the seat determine the splay of the legs and the lengths of the stretchers. The angles of the spindle sockets dictate how much the back will recline. The cant of the armposts results from the angles of the armpost sockets. This cant determines

the length of the armposts as well as the length of the arm.

The seat is the key to the legendary durability of Windsors. The two major systems of the chair, the back and undercarriage, are secured into this solid block of wood. The chair is engineered so that the parts of these systems are always pushing and pulling against each other. The seat is a reliable anchor that allows the chairmaker to strengthen the chair by placing its parts under tension in such a way that use tightens, rather than loosens, the joints.

The visual center of the chair is also the seat. By separating the back and the undercarriage, the seat prevents them from competing with each other and forces them to contribute instead to the artistic success of the chair. No matter where the viewer's eye is drawn by the sweeping curves of the back and its radiating spindles, or by the bold rake of the legs, it is pulled back by the robust and dynamic form of the seat.

Wood Selection

The seat should be made of wood that is lightweight, soft and stable, with little figure. I usually use eastern white pine. If you cannot get this species, you will probably want to work with one native to your area. When in the western United States, I have made seats of sugar pine and ponderosa pine. In Ohio, I have used tulip (also called yellow poplar), and find that an excellent wood. I have also used basswood, and even once made a set of chairs with Honduras-mahogany seats. A friend in Georgia makes seats of cypress. If you are using a local wood, avoid those that are difficult to excavate and sculpt, such as maple, birch, cherry, walnut, oak, ash and hickory.

I purchase 2-in.-thick, rough-sawn planks of white pine directly from the mill and air-dry them myself for at least one year. I do this because it is less costly, but kiln-dried wood will work fine, too. The planks will eventually be cut into short sections, so their length is not important. I try to buy wide planks that do not have too much sapwood, because pine heartwood is much easier to work. Clear planks would be ideal, but I usually end up sawing the seats out from between clusters of knots.

Wood constantly reacts to changes in humidity—shrinking when the weather is dry and swelling when it is wet. If you live in the Southwest, where the air is continually dry, or the Northwest, where it is always moist, the humidity probably does not change enough to affect your wood. If you live in the frost belt, like I do, you must be concerned with wood movement, because the humidity fluctuates widely. In the summer, when the humidity is high, we open our windows and allow the warm, moist air to move freely about. In the winter, we seal our houses and pump them full of hot, dry air. Wooden furniture is constantly swelling and shrinking in these conditions. This movement creates stresses that sometimes crack or check a chair's seat. The largest and longest checks will occur in seats made of single boards. A seat glued up of two or more pieces is more resistant to splitting because the stresses are broken by each joint.

My customers usually have a strong traditional bent and request a single-piece seat. Therefore, I usually work with a single piece of wood, even though I know it is not necessarily the best possible seat. The seat for the sack-back chair is 15¾ in. wide, the seat for the continuous-arm Windsor 18 in. wide. If I am out of 18-in. planks, I have no qualms about gluing a strip to one of the narrower planks. Only 2¼ in. is needed, but I usually add a wider strip to avoid boring an armpost socket through the glue joint. If you glue up seat blanks, make sure that the grain is running in the same direction on all the pieces. If the grain on one piece is rising and on the other dipping, any cut along the joint will tear, no matter which direction the tool is worked. When gluing, look at the mating edges of the boards and make sure that the slope of the grain on each is running in the same direction. Avoid any black knots, which may loosen in time. I occasionally work bright, also called live, knots. These will not loosen, but they do increase the amount of work needed to shape the seat.

The two most common Windsor-seat shapes are the oval, used here for the sack-back chair, and the shield, used for the continuous-arm chair. The grain of the oval seat runs from side to side; that of the shield seat runs from front to back. The sack back is a shallow yet commodious chair, the continuous arm is deep and supportive of the sitter's torso. All the techniques required to make the oval seat are used when making the shield, so I will describe how to make the shield seat first. Then I will outline the making of an oval seat, drawing your attention to any different processes needed.

1 *Clean up the rough faces of the seat blank so you can decide which is the best face for the top surface.*

Shield Seat

The shield seat requires a blank that is 18 in. square. If the chair is to have a back brace (two spindles connecting the bent back to a tailpiece on the seat), the seat blank should be 18 in. wide and 21 in. long to allow for the tailpiece. The brace is a desirable feature on the continuous-arm chair. Its bent back is anchored to only the armposts, and all the stress created when the chair is in use is transmitted to the spindles of the back. The brace regulates just how much the spindles can flex, and it transfers some of the stress down to the robust tailpiece.

The faces of a rough-sawn blank must be planed so that you can see the grain to judge which face will be the top of the seat. A thickness planer will do the job, but I do not have one, so I hand-plane the seat blanks (**1**). I use a wooden plane about 16 in. long, known as a jack plane or foreplane. The plane blade has a convex cutting edge that removes heavy, coarse shavings and quickly disposes of the rough surface.

After planing, inspect the surfaces and decide which will be the top. Do not be concerned with the direction in which the wood will cup if it should warp. The seat is so short in relation to its width, and its surface is so undulate that no one will notice. A lot of wood will be removed from the top surface of the seat, so place any spike knots, pitch pockets or other blemishes that do not run completely through the blank on the seat bottom, to avoid having to work them. Try to place through knots at the rear of the seat—you can probably arrange the spindles on either side of a knot. When you have chosen the top surface, plane it flat. I use a wooden smoothing plane with a straight, sharp cutting edge. Though most of this surface will be removed when the seat is excavated (or saddled), if it were not finish-planed, the tracks of the foreplane would remain where the spindles meet the seat.

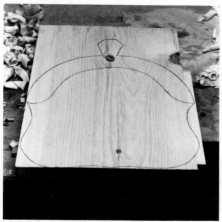

2 *Make a pattern for the seat out of heavy cardboard. If possible, position the pattern so that knots and other blemishes are out of the areas to be excavated.*

3 *A 25-in. bow saw makes short work of cutting out the seat. Clamp the blank securely to the bench. Saw with the full length of the blade and use your whole body, not just your arms, for the strokes.*

Next, make a pattern for the seat. Because I use my patterns over and over, I make them of heavy cardboard. The shape of the seat is shown on p. 141. To reproduce it full-scale, superimpose a grid of ¼-in. squares on the large plan drawing. Draw a grid of 1-in. squares on the cardboard, and reproduce the curve in each small square on the plan in the corresponding large square on the cardboard pattern. Mark the position of the sockets for the legs, armposts and spindles on the pattern. When you cut out the pattern, make sure that all the curves are smooth.

Trace the outline of the seat onto the blank (2). Pay attention to knots and blemishes when placing the pattern and, when possible, keep them out of the area that will be excavated. Draw in the carved channel that circumscribes the saddle and separates it from the spindles and posts. I draw this free-hand, judging the distance from the

back edge of the seat by eye. You could use dividers or a pattern if you do not trust your eye. I do not bother at this point to mark any of the sockets.

I cut out the seat with a 25-in. bow saw (3). It takes so little time to do this that I have never even been tempted to buy a bandsaw. I clamp the blank to the corner of a bench with wooden hand-screw clamps, and I saw right to the line—this saves clean-up later. I prefer hand-screw clamps with wooden screws to those with metal screws, because the wooden screws flex and can accept more torque. Their flexibility also gives the clamp a springlike quality. If the blank shifts and loosens the clamp slightly, the springy back screw will adjust for the slack, whereas a hand-screw clamp with metal screws will fall to the floor. There is only one drawback to an all-wood hand-screw clamp: The threads are vulnerable to damage from bumps and bangs. Screws

that have been damaged, however, can be discarded and new ones made with a screw box. With a threaded die and its corresponding tap (I use a ¾ in.), you can make all the clamps that you could possibly want or need.

Though I have seen it suggested that some excavating be done prior to cutting out the seat, I do not know any chairmakers who work this way. I prefer to do all operations that require the same tools at one time. When I am finished with the operation, I put the tools away and thus avoid a cluttered workbench (benches have a natural tendency to become cluttered).

4 *The edge of a Windsor seat is roughly shaped with a drawknife (left). Use as much of the drawknife blade as possible to make a slicing cut. Finish shaping the edge with spokeshaves and planes (facing page). The large and small spokeshaves can work concave as well as convex surfaces. The smoothing plane (far right) works convex surfaces and the compass plane (second from right) is useful for the incline along the front of the seat.*

Shaping the Edge

The first step in shaping the seat is to contour the edges. This contour is complex, changing several times as it moves around the outline of the seat, as shown in the photos and drawings in Chapter XII. Along the back and up to the armposts, the shape is very nearly a quarter round. Adjacent to the armposts, where the shield shape is indented, the edge changes abruptly. Here, a long, low incline beneath the indentation rises to meet the slightly sloping top surface of the seat. This incline on the seat bottom develops into a large-radius curve under the front corners of the seat. Between the corners, the bottom profile becomes an incline once again. A distinct arris runs around the edge from armpost to armpost, delineating the top and bottom surfaces and sharply defining the shape of the seat. I establish the line of the arris by eye while sculpting the seat. It might help you to sketch it on the edge with a pencil.

There are two steps in shaping the edge of a seat. First, remove the bulk of the waste with a drawknife. Second, finish the edge with spokeshaves and planes. I shape the edge in sections, moving back and forth between the drawknife, two spokeshaves, a smoothing plane and a compass plane (4). This alternation is merely my habit, and I urge you to find a way of working that is comfortable for you. Before describing the edge-shaping process, I will discuss the shaping tools.

Drawknife The general progression in most woodworking is to move from coarse tools that remove large amounts of wood through a series of increasingly refined tools that are easier to control. The coarse tool for this job is a drawknife. The one I use is a traditional Anglo-American pattern, 12 in. long overall, with a 7½-in.-long blade. A drawknife that is longer than this is awkward to control, and one that is shorter is too light and too short to take a complete cut. The handles are about 5 in. long and lie in the same plane as the blade. I find this tool easier to control than drawknives with handles that are offset from the blade. They have a tendency to dive into the grain. I have never been comfortable with Continental-style drawknives, which have egg-shaped handles.

When I use a drawknife, I grip it very securely. My wrists are stiff to prevent the tool from diving into the wood. Because I am right-handed, I hold the right handle closest to me. In this position, the blade slices through the wood at a skewed angle. As you work around the seat's outline, you move from edge grain into end grain and back into edge grain again. A skewed, slicing cut, using as much of the length of the blade as possible, is less likely to chatter or dig into end grain. Do not try to hew away the wood as if you were using a two-handled hatchet. When used properly, the drawknife will remove a lot of wood very quickly, and with a surprising amount of control.

I like to work the drawknife at about the height of my sternum. My elbows and shoulders act as a natural stop, so I do not worry about cutting myself. Each drawknife cut has three distinct motions. Begin the cut by gradually entering the blade into the wood. Slice through the shaving with a second, long motion. Then separate the shaving and end the cut. Most people have trouble with this third action. Think of it as you would the follow-through of a swing with a golf club or a baseball bat. You must follow through with edge tools to prevent digging and tearing the grain. This greatly reduces clean-up with abrasives and scrapers.

Spokeshaves and planes I finish shaping the edge with two wooden spokeshaves and two wooden planes. I like my tools to wear to fit the work they do. The sole of the wooden smoothing plane has a distinct hollow worn in front of the mouth, which helps the plane to track on a rounded surface. The small spokeshave has a wear spot on the sole where I whittle spindles. This wear spot also allows the tool to get down into a tight radius, such as in the concave area of the seat edge. The compass plane is shaped very much like the smoothing plane, but its sole is curved from front to back. I use it on the inclined front edge of the seat.

I prefer wooden spokeshaves to metal ones. A metal spokeshave is really a plane with two handles. The blade is set at 45° in the stock, bevel down. The sole has a mouth, just like the sole of a plane, as shown in the drawing at right. The blade is held in place by a set screw, which must be loosened and tightened during adjustment. A wooden spokeshave is a true shave. The blade is very nearly parallel to the sole, which means that it makes a paring cut, very much like the cut made by a knife or chisel. This paring cut is ideal for working end grain.

Spokeshaves

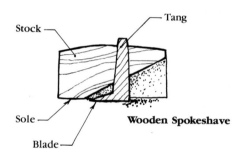

Wooden Spokeshave

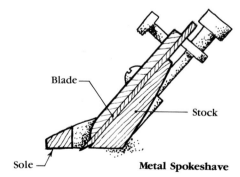

Metal Spokeshave

The blade has a tang at each end, bent at right angles to the length of the cutting edge. The tangs are press-fitted into holes in the stock. The depth of cut is increased by tapping the ends of the tangs and decreased by striking the flat of the blade beneath each tang. This tapping can be done on any handy surface, like the corner of a bench or the vise, so adjustments can be made quickly, with one hand.

For finishing the seat edge, I set the spokeshave blade by cocking the two tangs so that the blade protrudes beneath the sole farther at one end than at the other. By working back and forth along the length of the cutting edge, you can find just the right spot to cut a shaving of the thickness that you desire. With practice, selecting this spot becomes second nature.

5 *Rough-out the quarter round on the back edge of the seat with a drawknife.*

6 *Complete the quarter round with spokeshaves. Skew the small spokeshave to clean up the chatter marks on the end grain.*

Shaping I prefer to hold the seat in a vise while shaping most of the edge, keeping the area being worked more or less horizontal. Begin drawknifing with the quarter-round profile on the back edge. This shape can be roughed-out with drawknife cuts at three angles, as shown in the drawing at right. Make the first slice at about 45° from the perpendicular. This should be a heavy cut. In pine, I take off as much as ¾ in. (**5**). Now make two shallower cuts above and below the first cut and at a smaller angle. Be careful to leave some of the sawn edge near the top of the contour so that you do not lose the shape. The tailpiece creates two corners that are difficult to work. Slice up to it as closely as you can with the drawknife. The tailpiece and area adjacent to it will be finished later using a chisel. Work the quarter-round shape up to the position of the armpost on one side.

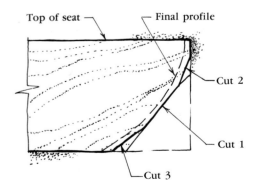

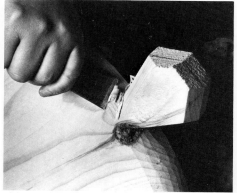

7 *Clean up the edges of the tailpiece and carve the bevels with a wide chisel. You can take a heavy cut when beveling (left). Trim the quarter-round back edge up to the bevel (top right). Grasp the tailpiece and chisel with one hand to help control the cut (bottom right).*

On an oval seat, or a shield seat with no tailpiece, I need only the smoothing plane to finish the quarter round. The surface is rough from the drawknife, and the plane brings it to the desired contour more quickly than even the large spokeshave. But the plane will bump into a tailpiece, so I use the large spokeshave when necessary to avoid this (**6**). Even this tool will not get down completely into the corner formed by the back of the seat and the tail. This area has to be cleaned up with a wide chisel. I do this when shaping the tailpiece.

The plane and large spokeshave are heavy tools, set to take a heavy cut. Therefore, they might dig in slightly on the end grain. These marks can be quickly cleaned up with the smaller spokeshave, which is easy to set for a fine cut. This tool is so light, however, that it will chatter as it hits the alternating hard late growth and soft early growth of the annual rings. To prevent this chattering, I skew the spokeshave at right angles to the rings, so that the cutting edge runs across several rings at a time and is not able to burrow into the softer areas.

When the rear edge is cleaned up, shape the tailpiece with a wide chisel. The lower edge of the tailpiece is beveled. I like this bevel to account for about three fifths of the thickness of the seat. This makes the tailpiece appear more three-dimensional and thinner than it really is. While working on the tailpiece, clean up the corners where the tailpiece meets the seat (**7**).

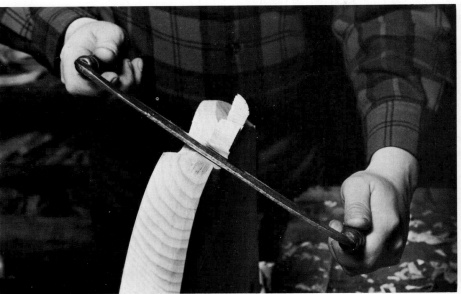

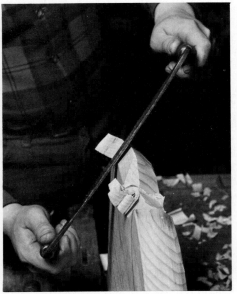

8 *To rough-out the edge in front of the armpost, first remove the arris at the front corner (top). Then shape the concavities at the indentation of the shield on both top and bottom surfaces (left). Finally, make a low-angled cut on the top surface at the corner (right).*

Next, shape the edge in front of the armpost. This area is complicated. It may help you to refer frequently to the photos and drawings in Chapter XII when reading the description, and when making the seat. Where the shield shape is indented, the top surface of the seat slopes slightly down, meeting a long, low, slightly convex incline rising from the bottom. This bottom incline develops into a large-radius curve under the front corners of the seat. The top surface of the corner is also a slight, convex slope.

First, make a heavy 45° cut with the drawknife to remove the bottom arris of the front corner of the seat (**8**). The shield indentation is perhaps the most difficult area of the seat to clean up, because end grain is exposed on both sides of the concave curves. Cut down the sides toward the bottom of the curve with the drawknife. If you cut upward, the cutting edge will get buried in the end grain.

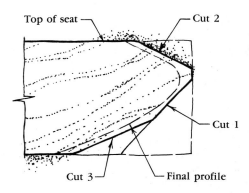

9 Use the large and small spokeshaves to continue roughing-out the edge profile for the shield indentation and the front corner.

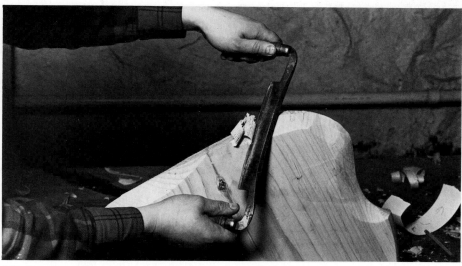

10 Rough-out the incline along the front edge with the drawknife.

Rough-out the rest of the front corner. You have made the first cut, eliminating the bottom arris. A second cut, below the first, should be at a shallower angle, as shown in the drawing at left. A third cut removes the upper corner.

Continue work on the edge with the large and small spokeshaves (9). A lot of wood needs to be removed from both top and bottom surfaces in the shield indentation and the front corner. I remove as much as possible now, but leave the final shaping until later when the seat is flat on the benchtop.

Next, begin the incline in front. Shape the incline with a series of slicing cuts at 45°, as shown in the drawing at right. Usually, I can work only as far as the pommel without changing the position of the seat in the vise.

About half of the seat edge is roughly to shape now. The seat is symmetrical, so follow the same process on the other half. When I switch the seat around in the vise to work on the concave area of the opposite side, I am able to finish cutting away the rest of the front edge profile at the same time (10).

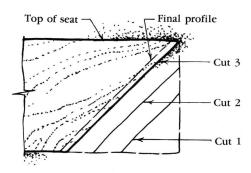

Top of seat — Final profile
— Cut 3
— Cut 2
— Cut 1

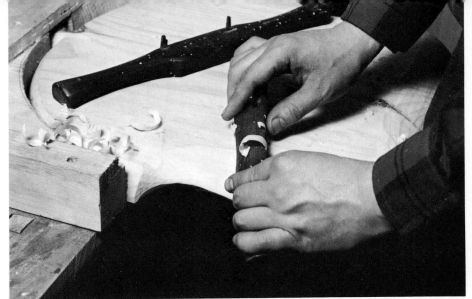

12 *Shape the curve under each shield indentation carefully. Work the spokeshave with the grain so that it won't dig in. This small spokeshave fits curves of a smaller radius than the large one in the background.*

11 *A simple wooden frame will hold the seat on the bench while shaping. Two threaded wooden screws fit through the back of the frame into the benchtop. Bore and tap a series of holes in the benchtop so that the frame can be positioned for several different jobs.*

Finish-shaping Take the seat from the vise and place it upside down on the bench. I have made a frame to hold the seat on the bench for shaping (**11**). The remainder of the edge-shaping, most of the saddling on the top surface and all of the socket-boring are done with the seat held in the frame.

The frame is designed to hold the seat by gripping the tailpiece, and either the top or bottom surface of the seat can be placed up. The frame is secured to the bench with two threaded wooden screws, for which you will need a screw box and tap. These come in sets of various sizes—a ¾-in. set will do for the frame as well as for making wooden hand-screw clamps. Several rows of threaded holes in the benchtop permit positioning the frame appropriately for different tasks. When shaping

the edge, the front half of the seat should extend beyond the benchtop so that the edge can be easily worked. Two hand-screw clamps, carefully placed so that the jaws grip the seat along the back edge, will also work. If you are clamping, place the seat on the corner of the benchtop so that the two shield indentations overhang and give plenty of free space in which to work.

Finish shaping the bottom inclines at the indentations on each side of the shield with the small spokeshave (**12**). As mentioned earlier, the grain changes direction in this area, so it is necessary to cut from back to center and front to center to avoid digging into the grain.

Proper completion of this shape is important. The continuous-arm Windsor is a delicate and complex chair, a symphony of curves. The seat is a block of wood in the center of a sensuous, undulate form. If it reads as a static lump, the visual success of the chair is impaired. When the chair is viewed from the side, the long slope of the incline on the bottom of the seat makes it appear thinner than it really is. This illusion of thinness is important. However, you must make sure that it is only an illusion; if the seat is too thin where the leg and arm sockets are, the chair will be weak. An ample amount of wood must remain at the joints, but the shaping of the seat between these points must flow naturally.

13 *Complete the incline along the front edge of the seat with a compass plane.*

14 *Clean up torn end grain and make the transitions from one profile to another flow smoothly together with a spokeshave.*

With the seat upside down, I complete the incline along the front edge with a compass plane (**13**). This tool, with its curved sole, creates a gentle concavity across the lower front edge. (If you do not have a compass plane, a large spokeshave can be used to give the same effect.) Because the plane blade is set at 45°, it will often tear out the soft early growth, so this surface should be cleaned up with the small spokeshave using the same skew technique described earlier.

While I have the spokeshave in hand, I make all the transitions flow together—from the incline of the front into the radius of the corners and from the corners into the incline under the indented edges (**14**).

The bottom of the seat is now finished. The planes, spokeshaves and chisel each leave their own individual track. You may wish to sand these out, and can do so quite easily because the evidence of good handwork is subtle. However, I am neither ashamed of nor offended by these tracks, and they remain on any chair I make.

15 *Stand on the seat to hold it when using the adze. Swing the adze with your wrists and follow through the stroke to sever the chip. Work with the grain, from each end of the seat into the center, where the saddling is deepest.*

Saddling

After shaping the edge, the top surface of the seat needs to be excavated. The area where this is to be done begins at the line for the carved channel and continues to the front edge of the chair. The completed shape looks like a saddle, so the process is often called saddling. The tool used to cut away the majority of the waste is the gutter adze (**15**). (I bought my gutter adze used, but used ones are rare. Similar adzes are made today, but I find their curves less satisfactory than mine. The tool would not be too difficult to make, and a pattern is shown at right.) If you do not have a gutter adze, there are other ways of doing its work, but these require more time and effort. You could remove waste from the saddled area with a heavy gouge and mallet. You could also use a sculptor's one-handed adze. This is not as heavy as the gutter adze and will not work as quickly. You could also do all of the saddling with the scorp (p. 16). If you opt for any of these other tools, you will want to work with the seat secured to the benchtop.

Gutter-Adze Pattern

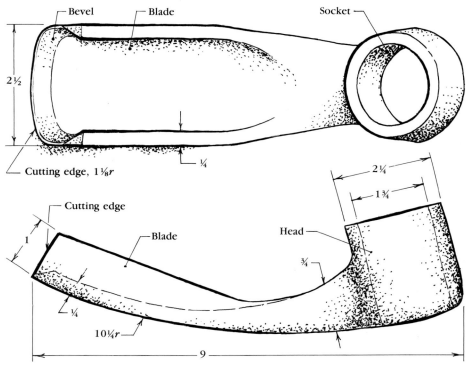

Bevel Blade Socket

$2\frac{1}{2}$

Cutting edge, $1\frac{1}{8}r$

$\frac{1}{4}$

Cutting edge

Blade Head

$2\frac{1}{4}$

$1\frac{3}{4}$

1

$\frac{3}{4}$

$\frac{1}{4}$

$10\frac{1}{4}r$

9

Note: *All dimensions are approximate.*

16 *If you are confident, you can use the adze close to the outline of the saddled area, as shown at left. Reverse the seat to hew along the front, as shown at right.*

The business end of the gutter adze is curved, and can take a thick, narrow chip in a relatively small, but deeply concave area. An adze with a wider, less curved blade would be awkward to use, because it could not get into the curves of the saddle. The length of the adze handle is important. The saddled area is no more than 1½ sq. ft., and I stand on the seat while using the adze. For both the sake of safety and the job, it is essential to use the gutter adze as accurately as possible. I have hafted my adze with an oak handle that is only 17 in. long, which allows me to swing the adze with my wrists, and keep the tool close to the work. If the handle were longer, I could not achieve the unfailing accuracy needed to chop out a seat. Even so, I wear steel-toed shoes.

Place the seat on the floor. I like to stand on it rather than hold it with the sides of my feet or ankles—my weight holds the seat immobile, and I do not have to worry about the adze missing and hitting a part of me that is not well protected. Work the adze with the grain, using short strokes. As with most hand tools, it is important to follow through with these strokes and completely separate the chip from the seat. This leaves no digs to be removed with finishing tools. Resist the temptation to break a chip loose by lifting it rather than cutting it away, because the chip might split out and run right out the other end of the piece. You might practice on a piece of scrap until you are comfortable with the adze. Used incorrectly, it can ruin your seat.

Work about half the saddled area, beginning at one end of the seat and moving toward the center. Then start at the opposite end, again chopping toward the center (16). Remove any high spots left in the center by chopping in from both directions with the grain.

The purpose of the gutter adze is to remove a lot of waste very quickly. No real shaping is done with the adze, and the seat surface will be very rough. Where the saddle is deepest, the dished area in the center of the seat, I remove at least ⅝ in. from a 2-in.-thick seat. The more waste that can be removed with the adze, the less there will be to remove with lightweight tools. The next step will clean up the rugged depression and begin to give some form to the seat. The tool used for this is the scorp.

Sculpting the Seat **15**

17 *The smooth surface at the back of the seat has been worked with the scorp, after the entire saddle has been adzed roughly to shape. When smoothing, work the scorp from the back to the center of the saddle.*

19 *Work the pommel area with a small spokeshave skewed to the grain direction.*

18 *Blend the area in front of the armposts into the saddle with the scorp. Cut at an angle to the grain, not across it.*

Though the scorp is a hollowing tool, it is essentially a bent drawknife. It is a basic instrument, in that the only control is in the user's wrists. Because the scorp does not have a mouth to regulate the depth of cut as does a plane or spokeshave, it is not the tool I choose for finishing. This lack of a mouth, however, allows the scorp to remove a lot of wood very quickly.

The scorp I use has a blade that is bent to a radius (17). Many scorps, both modern and antique, are *U*-shaped with a flat bottom. This flat-bottomed type seems to have been designed for coopers. It is nearly useless for chairmaking, because it does not allow you to get down into the saddle.

To use the scorp, I secure the seat to the bench with the hold-down frame. As with a drawknife, a scorp is pulled and performs best when the cutting edge is skewed to the grain direction. Control the tool with your wrists to take either heavy chips or light shavings. Follow through each cut with an upward flick of the wrists to separate the chip completely and prevent the edge from digging in.

First, cut away large pieces of wood to clean up the work done by the adze. Then use the scorp to bring the saddled area to almost its finished depth. Hold the ends of the handles about 1 in. above the seat to remove wood aggressively and efficiently. Cut from the rear to the center of the seat. If you go any farther, you will dig into the rising grain. Work also from the front to the center. I do this by sitting on the bench, so that I do not have to reverse the hold-down frame. Be careful not to remove too much wood from the areas where the leg sockets are to be bored.

When working the edge of the seat, some shaping was done on the concave area in front of where the armposts will be. Now use the scorp to blend this area into the saddle (18).

On the oval seat, the pommel can be shaped with the scorp, because the grain runs from side to side, and you can cut with the grain. The pommel of a shield seat is worked across the grain, and as a result, this has to be done with the small spokeshave (19). To perform best, the spokeshave should be skewed to the growth rings, forming an X with them if possible. Cut mostly away from the pommel, working from the center to the sides of the seat. This creates a sharp peak that is a distraction on a seat that is otherwise made up of gentle curves. I soften the peak by running the spokeshave right over it, turning it into a swelling. While working in this area, flow the curve of the corners into the edge on either side of the pommel.

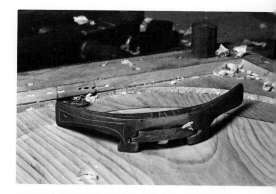

20 *The final shaping tool for the saddle is the miniature compass plane, which has a curved sole. The cutting edge is ground slightly convex so that it will not dig in. Nest the compass plane in both hands and work in the direction of the grain.*

21 *The travisher smooths the furrows left on the saddle by the compass plane. It has a curved, wooden frame and a curved blade that cuts like a spokeshave. Push the travisher with rigid wrists. Work with or skewed to the grain into the center of the seat.*

The surface left by the scorp will still be rough and will require further work. I use a miniature compass plane first to take out any unevenness left by the scorp (**20**). Like the larger compass plane used earlier, the sole of this little plane is also curved from end to end, which allows it to work in an indentation. The one I use is wooden and only 5 in. long and 1½ in. wide. It is small enough to get down into the deepest part of the seat. As with the foreplane, I grind a convex cutting edge on the blade so that it can take a heavy chip without digging into the wood. The compass plane's depth of cut is regulated—the plane will cut only as deep as the blade is set, no matter how much force or pressure is used.

The operation of this plane is fairly simple. Nest it in both hands, holding your wrists rigid. The secret of its successful use is to follow through with each cut. A short, choppy motion will dig into the wood rather than smooth it. I clean up the dished area first, working back to center and front to center, as with the scorp. Then, I blend the saddle into the seat's outline.

The seat has now taken its final form and needs only to be smoothed. The surface is still somewhat rough because the convex cutting edge of the compass plane leaves a distinctly furrowed track, which should be removed. The tool that does this work is, as far as I know, unique to chairmaking. It is called a travisher, and it looks like a bent spokeshave (**21**). Indeed, the travisher works in the same manner as a spokeshave. The curve allows it to clean up hollowed surfaces.

Hold your wrists rigid when using the travisher. It is a light tool, set to take a very light cut. Its own weight is insufficient to keep it from wobbling or chattering. If you push it, you can put more weight behind the tool, which will help it cut cleanly. Once again, follow the strokes through and end each stroke with an upward flick of the wrists. This completely separates the shaving and eliminates the digs caused by an incomplete stroke.

Work the travisher with the grain, from the front and back of the seat, moving toward the center. In the middle of the seat, at the bottom of the depression, the travisher sometimes tears. This is because it is cutting into the grain that runs up the opposite slope of the saddle. This awkward grain can usually be taken care of with very short, light strokes. If the tearing persists, however, you can eliminate it by working across the grain. This will create some roughness that will need to be sanded away.

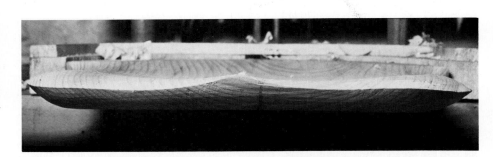

22 *Finish the gently rolled edge of the front corners with a small spokeshave.*

23 *The shaping of the seat is complete when the furrows have been smoothed out and the curves flow into each other.*

I know of no manufacturer who is making the small compass plane and the travisher today. I bought my compass plane used and made my travisher. (I cut the travisher's curved, wooden body out of a solid piece of wood and had a blacksmith make a bent spokeshave blade to match.) Until I discovered these tools, I finished the saddling with the scorp. To do this, lower the handles until their ends almost drag on the surface of the wood. The scorp will now scrape rather than cut. Work it skewed to the grain for a more acceptable surface. A seat that has been finished with the scorp will require more sanding than one finished with a compass plane and travisher.

Some areas of the seat are flat enough to be smoothed with the travisher's cousin, the spokeshave. The pronounced dip along the edges of the seat between the armposts and the front corners is more easily worked with the spokeshave than the travisher. I also prefer to finish the gently rolled edge of the front corners with the spokeshave, using the part of the blade that is set to take a fine cut (**22**).

The shaping of the seat is now complete. The curves should be crisp and flow gracefully from one side to the other (**23**). If they do, the seat will echo the bold curves of the back.

Next, carve the channel that outlines the dished area along the back of the seat. This detail separates the two distinct areas of the top surface—the saddle and the flat area where the sockets are bored. It also makes the transition between them smoother. I make the channel with a ¼-in. veiner (**24**). You can extend the channel around the arris of the rear edge of the seat if you wish; I prefer to bevel it with a spokeshave. Run the channel or bevel around the tailpiece as well.

24 *Carve the channel that separates the excavated saddle from the flat surface at the back of the seat with a ¼-in. veiner.*

25 *Sand the seat with 50-grit sandpaper. Do not lose the sharp arris on the edge.*

I sand the seat with only a quarter sheet of 50-grit sandpaper (**25**). This removes any roughness that might remain after smoothing with the travisher. I do not spend a lot of time sanding now because the seat will be bumped and banged and have glue spilled on it as the chair is put together. After the chair is completed, I moisten the saddled area with a sponge. This raises the grain as well as any scratches made by the 50-grit paper. When the saddle has dried, I sand with 120-grit paper.

26 *Trace the pattern for the oval seat onto the blank. Add lines for the carved channel, the pommel and the ridges between the pommel and the armposts.*

27 *Rough-out the quarter-round profile of the edge with a drawknife.*

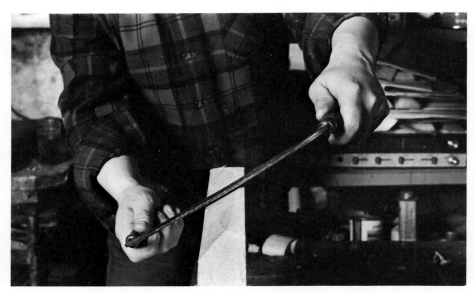

28 *The front edge of the seat beneath the pommel is an incline, which can be roughed-out quickly with four or five drawknife cuts at about a 40° angle.*

Oval Seat

The oval seat is a much simpler shape than the shield seat, and consequently it is easier to make. Select the wood for the oval seat using the same criteria as for the shield seat. The blank should be at least 21 in. long and 15¾ in. wide; the grain runs from side to side of the chair. Make a pattern for the seat by scaling up the drawing on p. 133. Clean off one face of the blank with the foreplane and smooth it with a smoothing plane. Then trace around the pattern.

Mark the carved channel that separates the sculpted part of the seat from the flat area that wraps around about three quarters of the edge. The ends of the flat area are straight, and are indicated by the line running from side to side across the seat in photo **26**. Mark the exact middle of the front curve, which is the location of the pommel, and extend the line of the carved channel out to meet this point. These lines indicate ridges that delineate the extent of the dished area in the center of the seat, and from them the seat will slope gently down to the front edge.

Cut out the seat, then rough-out the shape of the edge with the drawknife. The edge profile is a quarter round to the middle of the front edge (**27**), where it breaks gently into an incline of about 40° with little or no curve (**28**). Both shapes are easily roughed-out with the drawknife, as shown in the drawings on pp. 8 and 11.

30 *The rough quarter-round profile on the right side of the photo is planed and spokeshaved to an even, uniform curve, as shown at left.*

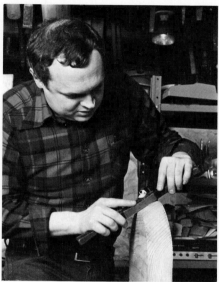

29 *Finish the quarter-round curve along the back edge of the seat with a smoothing plane or large spokeshave. The soles of these tools have worn slightly hollow, which helps them track on the edge.*

31 *Rough-out the top surface with a gutter adze, working into the middle. Sever a chip with each swing—don't pry it up.*

I prefer to do most of the finish-shaping of the oval-seat edge with the smoothing plane (**29**). The quarter-round edge is faceted by the drawknife, and the plane can bring it to the desired contour more quickly than even the large spokeshave. With the small spokeshave, clean up any spots where the plane blade has dug into the end grain (**30**). The incline along the front can also be finished with the smoothing plane, then make the transition from the quarter round to the incline with the spokeshave. The transition occurs beneath where the sitter's legs extend over the seat. All the edge-shaping so far can be done with the seat held vertically in a vise.

After shaping the edge, place the seat on the floor and hew out the top surface with the gutter adze (**31**). This is done in the same manner as for the shield seat, except that you should swing the adze from each side of the seat toward the center, because the grain runs side to side. Hew up to the curved ridge lines drawn between the pommel and the corners of the channel. This gentle ridge will remain after the saddle is complete. If you feel confident of your ability, you can rough-out some of the slope that runs down from the ridge to the seat edge. If not, wait and remove this wood with the scorp.

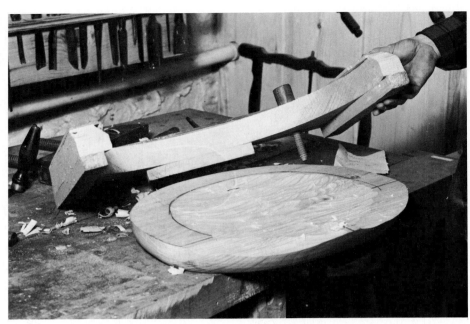

32 *This hold-down frame is shaped to fit the oval seat and is fixed to the benchtop with threaded wooden screws.*

33 *Work the dished area and the areas around the ridges to their final shape and depth with the scorp.*

When you are finished with the adze, secure the seat to the bench with a hold-down frame similar to that used for the shield seat, or clamps (32). If you clamp, place the seat over a corner so you will have access to more of the seat's circumference.

Work the dished area with the scorp. Cut aggressively and take out heavy chips—clean up the adze marks as quickly as you can. While working in this fashion, rough-out the slopes of the ridge if you did not do this with the adze. The ridge serves two functions. The two front-leg sockets are bored near it, so the ridge assures ample thickness for a strong joint. The ridge also creates an edge on the dished area. A sitter can sense this and does not feel that it is possible to slide forward and out of the chair.

The three areas on the top surface— the dished area and the slopes down from the ridges on either side of the pommel—should be worked more carefully with the scorp to bring them to their final shape and depth (33). I finish the surfaces with the compass plane, travisher and small spokeshave, as described for the shield seat (34). You can scrape with the scorp if you do not have one or more of these tools.

34 *Finish dishing with a compass plane and travisher, or scrape with a scorp.*

35 *Work a small spokeshave with the grain to shape the pommel.*

36 *The completed oval seat has a distinct arris along the front edge, sharply defining the top and bottom surfaces of the seat. A ridge on either side of the pommel separates the dished area from a gentle slope down to the front arris.*

Take some care with the final shaping of the ridges and the surfaces that slope from them. If the ridges are too sharp or too pronounced, they risk cutting off the circulation of blood to the sitter's legs. I gently round the ridges with the small spokeshave.

Shape the pommel by working away from it toward both sides with the spokeshave (**35**). The tool will cut cleanly with the grain. I soften the peak of the pommel by running the shave over it. Later, I round it some more with 50-grit sandpaper. Finish the shaping of the oval seat by carving the channel with a ¼-in. veiner (**36**). You can continue the channel around the back edge of the seat, or simply bevel that arris with a spokeshave, as I do.

Chapter II

Windsor-Chair Joints

Windsor chairs are held together by socketed construction: cylindrical tenons fit into cylindrical mortises, or sockets. There are two types of socket joints, blind and through, and I use both in my chairs. The names of these joints are self-explanatory—the blind socket does not go through the piece, the through socket does. Blind socket joints are the simplest. They rely only on glue and the tight fit of the tenon in the socket to hold them together. Through socket joints can be strengthened by driving a wedge into the exposed end of the tenon. The wedge expands the end and prevents the tenon from being withdrawn.

Both of these simple joints are used in the backs of the continuous-arm and the sack-back chairs. The spindles are set in blind sockets in the seats and wedged into through sockets in the bent backs (**1**). More important are the socket joints that fix the legs to the seat and the stretchers to the legs and to each other. I use a blind socket joint and a through socket joint that are specially suited for these connections. Because these joints are so important, it is worth examining how they work.

Chairmakers have long relied on socket joints because they can be made very quickly. The sockets can be made with a brace and bit. The bit makes a hole of exactly the same diameter each time it is used, and by scribing a line on the bit, each socket can be made to the same depth. Tenons can be easily whittled or turned on a lathe.

The ease with which socket joints can be made is, however, their only advantage. Socket joints are not the best way in which to secure two parts together. In fact, in the whole spectrum of ways in which wood is joined, there are few that are less satisfactory. As surely as wood shrinks and swells in reaction to the moisture in the air, a socket joint will loosen. It will loosen no matter what is done to prevent it from doing so. A nail, screw or dowel driven into the joint only prevents it from coming apart. These fasteners cannot keep the joint tight. More esoteric solutions, such as compressing an oversized tenon before inserting it into the socket, or injecting a liquid to swell loose tenons, do not last much longer.

The search for an ideal socket joint—one that would never loosen—is doomed to failure by the nature of the material. So, why not use a socket joint capable of automatically tightening itself after changes in humidity have caused it to loosen? A through socket joint with tapered sockets and tenons does just that, and its properties are tailor-made for the leg-to-seat joint, one of the most important on the chair. I have found this joint on hundreds of eighteenth-century Windsors that are still in good working order.

1 *The bottom ends of the spindles are blind-socketed into the seat, as shown in the cross sections at left. The top ends are through-socketed and wedged into the bent bow or arm, as shown at right.*

2 *The legs and seat are joined by through socket joints that are tapered and wedged.*

Through Socket Joints

The socket and tenon of a tapered, through socket joint are truncated cones that taper at exactly the same angle, so the two parts nest perfectly and are self-centering. If the degree of the taper is within a certain range of angles, the friction between the parts will lock them together. This is the principle of the self-holding or locking taper systems that machinists know by such names as Morse, Jacobs, and Brown and Sharps. Locking tapers are also used by coopers to secure bungs and spigots in wooden barrels. You are likely to have encountered the locking taper in the drive center of a wood-turning lathe, or the chuck of a drill press. You know how effectively these parts are held in place if you have ever had to remove them. The shank of the lathe drive center, for example, is usually shaped to a locking taper of the Morse type. The shank fits into a tapered socket in the drive spindle of the headstock. Pressure on the drive center locks it into the spindle. This friction bond is strong. To break it and loosen the center, you must insert a drift pin into the rear of the spindle and give the pin a sharp rap.

The tapered sockets and tenons that join the legs and the seat of a Windsor lock in the same way (**2**). Although these joints are also glued and wedged, nothing will spare them from inevitably loosening as the wood swells and shrinks with changes in humidity. However, each time someone sits in the chair, the tenons are driven back into the tapered sockets and relocked. The beauty of this joint is that use, which wears out all other types of chairs, works to hold a Windsor together.

Tapered tenons and sockets are easy to make. The tenons are turned to shape in the lathe. The sockets are bored with a brace and spoon bit, then tapered with a tool called a reamer. A reamer resembles a steel cone that has been sliced in half along its axis; the two exposed edges are sharpened by beveling them toward the inside of the cone. My reamer tapers a socket at about 7°. (Wood has different properties than steel, so the angle of the taper is not as critical as for tapers used by machinists.) I generally turn the tenons so that their taper is slightly shallower than those of the sockets. Wedging the tenon at assembly spreads the tenon

and makes it conform to the socket. This allows a considerable margin of error when turning the tenons, so gauging the size and taper by eye is quite feasible. (See Chapters III and IV for how to make the joint.)

Of course, you can use a straight, through socket joint to fix the legs to the seat. I make a shoulder on a straight tenon, so that only the tenon can enter the socket. Undercutting the socket opening to house this shoulder will make a more presentable joint. At assembly, I wedge the tenon, just as for the tapered joint. This makes a good glue bond. But more important, the wedge prevents the tenon from retracting even when the joint eventually loosens—the tenon is permanently trapped between the shoulder and the flared top created by the wedge. At worst, a loose, wedged through tenon will rattle and twist in its socket. You can minimize the potential for twisting by using a wedge that is wider than the diameter of the tenon. The edges of the wedge will key into the soft pine of the seat and prevent the shaft from turning.

Blind Socket Joints

A blind socket is simply a hole bored partway into, but not through, the chair part. The tenon, which is turned or whittled to the diameter of the bit used to bore the socket, is glued into the socket. Glue is the only thing that secures the joint. When the glue bond fails, so does the joint.

The stretchers of many types of chairs are blind-socketed into the legs, and here is where most of these chairs usually first come apart. As a result, much attention has been paid to these joints. Manufacturers have devised super glues, wood swellers and tenon compressors in an effort to find a way to overcome the tendency of wooden chairs to fail at these points. These joints have long baffled anyone who has tried to keep them from loosening.

The stretchers of Windsors are blind-socketed into each other and into the legs. Although nothing can overcome the innate weaknesses of any socket joint, I combat the tendency of these blind socket joints to loosen in two ways. First, I make each of the three stretchers a bit long. The stretchers, therefore, push the legs apart rather than attempt to hold them together. The glue bond in the blind sockets will eventually break, but the joints will not loosen because the pushing keeps the joints perpetually under compression. The system works because the legs are anchored in the solid-wood seat. It is reliable because the locking, tapered joints are renewed each time someone sits in the chair.

The second technique is less reliable; it is no more than an insurance policy against loosening. I use it because it is simple and can be done quickly. The technique makes use of the shrinkage of green wood as it dries to lock a shaped tenon in place. To understand how this works, first consider what happens when you turn a leg or stretcher from a piece of straight-grained, riven green wood. As the part dries, its cross section changes from circular to oval.

The widest axis of the oval will be perpendicular to the growth rings. I locate the socket where one end of this wide axis will be, so that the axis of the socket and of the greatest shrinkage coincide. (On oak, this direction is parallel to the direction of the rays, which can be seen on the end of the piece.) As the leg or stretcher dries, its socket will shrink tightly around the tenon.

Leg and Stretcher Sockets

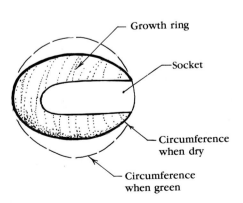

Locate a socket at a right angle to the growth rings to take advantage of the shrinkage of green-wood.

3 *The cross sections show how a socket in green wood will shrink around a dry, shaped tenon to form a locking joint. This shrinkage occurs only across the grain direction (center), not in line with it (left).*

To gain the most advantage from the shrinking socket, I shape the tenons of the stretchers to form two lobes. I first noticed this type of tenon years ago when repairing old ladder-back chairs. It can be made quickly and with precision. The tenon is first turned to a diameter just slightly exceeding that of the bit used to bore the socket. Then, two grooves are turned on it with a small gouge. The first groove is right next to the shoulder, making a distinct neck. The second is about halfway down the tenon's length. When the tenon is inserted into its socket, the walls of the socket will shrink around it and conform to the shape of the tenon, developing a locking ring around each of the two grooves in the tenon (**3**).

A problem arises here because both the tenoned and the socketed parts of the joint are made of green wood. Logic tells us that putting a wet tenon into a wet socket will only result in both drying and shrinking together. Ideally, a dry tenon should be inserted into a green socket. But the legs and side stretchers not only have tenons on one or both ends, they also have sockets bored somewhere along their lengths. The difficulty is how to dry the tenon while retaining enough moisture around the socket so it will shrink as it seasons. My solution is to immerse the tenon in a pot full of hot sand just before assembling the joint. The sand dries the tenon, but does not affect the moisture in the rest of the part.

The technique of inserting a dry, grooved tenon into a green socket can not keep a socketed joint tight forever. However, when the joint inevitably loosens, the locking ring will prevent it from coming apart. The tenon will rattle within the socket, but usually will not be able to move out of the ring. Combining this technique with the method of putting the joints in compression goes a long way toward ensuring a long life for the chair.

Turning the Legs

The undercarriage of a Windsor chair consists of the legs and stretchers. These parts are split from unseasoned logs, then turned on the lathe while they are still green. I will discuss how to split the wood first, then how to turn the parts.

Riving

I suggest that you split, or rive, all the turning stock for the chair. Most people have split wood for the stove, but riving differs from making stove wood in that the placement and direction of the split are controlled. Strength is one reason why I recommend riving. In a riven turning blank, the split follows the direction of the grain, so all the wood fibers in the blank run from one end of the piece to the other. Riven wood is therefore tough and capable of flexing.

Had the turning blank been sawn, the cut would have run in a straight line, ignoring the direction of the grain. A turning made from sawn wood risks having its grain run out at a narrow point, as shown below. When the leg is under stress, the wood may break along the grain at that point. Repair of such a break is nearly impossible. A riven turning will not fail in this way. If abused beyond what it can tolerate, a piece of riven stock will shear perpendicular to the grain. All its fibers will be severed, and the break will be at a right angle to the length of the turning.

Another reason why I recommend riving is economy. Riving is an ancient technique (the word is of archaic Scandinavian origin) and it is a wasteful one when judged by industrial standards. Although it is very efficient in its labor requirement, it is very inefficient in its consumption of materials. It would never be an acceptable general method in today's woodworking industry. However, when purchased in the log, wood is so cheap that people who are not mass-producing chairs can afford to rive stock and still come out ahead. Hardwood sells for more than a dollar a board

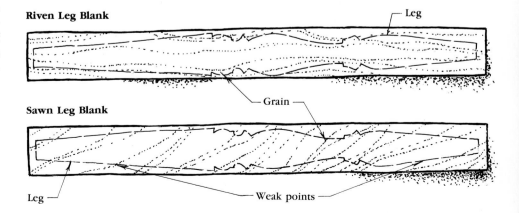

Riven Leg Blank

Leg

Grain

Sawn Leg Blank

Leg

Weak points

foot. Why pay this kind of money to a lumber dealer when superior stock is readily available in most unseasoned cord wood? I purchase the green wood I need for the undercarriage and backs of my chairs in logs from the same fellow who brings me my firewood. A lot of my riven wood is unusable for chair parts, but because I heat with wood, nothing is wasted. What comes into the shop on Monday goes out on Friday as a chair or in a bucket of ashes.

Wood selection A good baluster leg of the design I make has sharp, crisp details, and the wood I choose to turn must be able to render such results. I am fortunate to live in northern New England, an area that is still covered with hardwood forests. Obtaining wood is no problem for me, and I have been able to experiment with most of the common species. Through a process of elimination, I have selected two kinds of wood, red maple and paper birch, for chair legs and stretchers. (Red maple is a soft maple; paper birch is also called white birch.)

I have several reasons for preferring these woods. Both are common and easily obtained. Both split quickly and cleanly. They are not coarse and open-grained as are some other woods used in chairmaking, such as oak, ash or hickory. They are dense, diffuse-porous woods, so they will cut cleanly in the lathe and allow me to make good, crisp details. Maple and birch have a creamy color and smooth, clear consistency, so legs turned from them will not have pronounced figure that competes with the shape I turn for the viewer's attention. Depending on your location, you may or may not be able to obtain birch or maple. If not, you will have to experiment with species that are native to your region to find one that has these same properties.

I order wood in logs 5 ft. long. The longest turnings I make are chair legs, which are turned from 19½-in.-long blanks. If I allow for two chainsaw cuts, a 5-ft. log will render three sections of turning stock for legs and stretchers. (Five feet is also a good length for the oak logs from which I rive chair backs. The longest pieces needed are 58 in., for the continuous-arm chair.)

I like to work with logs from trees that grew in the forest and not by themselves. I also want them to be no less than 12 in. in diameter. Trees that grow in the open do not have to compete for sunlight with surrounding trees. Such trees do not usually produce good straight trunks, free of low limbs that form knots. To understand why forest-grown trees less than 12 in. in diameter are also unacceptable, it is necessary to know a bit about how trees grow.

Most of our forests are second growth; that is, the trees have reclaimed land that was originally forested, but was cleared for cultivation generations ago. If you look at photographs of the New England countryside taken late last century, you will be struck by the lack of trees. As the region became industrially developed, however, the farmers went to work in factories, abandoning the fields. The untilled land was very quickly reclaimed by the forests.

1 *For making chair legs, first cut the log into billets about 20 in. long.*

Maples and birches are called invading species because they are among the first to grow when an open space is left fallow. There are no adult trees for the first saplings to compete with. Consequently, these saplings are not forced to grow straight and tall to find sunlight in the openings of the forest canopy. Instead, they branch early. As the trees increase in size, however, they must compete with each other for sunlight. The trunk and upper branches shoot up. The lower limbs die and what remains of these branches is encased deep in the trunk near the heart. Wood that grows over the remains is deflected. This early growth, near the heart, is too twisted to rive and turn cleanly. Later growth, however, is less disturbed by the remains of the old branches, and this growth is eventually laid on smooth and straight. Several inches of growth out from the heart is necessary before this outer, superior wood can develop. I split turning blanks from this outer wood, and toss the heart into the stove. A log larger than 12 in. in diameter usually contains more usable wood.

A log for chairmaking should, therefore, have nearly perfectly straight grain, free of knots and twists. Such flaws make a log difficult to rive, and parts made from its wood tend to be weak. An acceptable log will split cleanly in two with a wedge and maul.

Determining whether a log is worth buying for chairmaking takes practice. Here are some outward signs that I look for. You can obtain a pretty good idea of the surprises that a log may contain inside by first examining its bark. Any bumps indicate an encased knot that is fairly close to the surface. I pass such logs by. Clear logs are easy enough to get that I don't mess with any with possible defects. Detecting deeper knots requires closer observation. Paper birch takes its name from the characteristics of its bark, which is as smooth and as white as writing paper. Where the tree has healed over a knot or other blemish, a black or dark grey whorl will appear on the bark. This whorl indicates that the log contains a defect that will make the wood useless for riving into turning blanks.

The bark of red maple is a little more difficult to describe, because it can vary so much from tree to tree. On younger trees, it can be grey and as smooth as birch. Any encased knots or other internal problems make themselves known by the pronounced effects they have on this smooth bark. The effects are similar to those described earlier for birch. On old trees, the bark is very coarse and a grey-brown color. When the tree is felled, skidded and loaded, the bark is abraded. Any high spots that indicate the presence of an encased knot will be rubbed until they are a distinctive brown—about the color of a pair of undyed leather shoes. The coarse bark also contains fissures that normally run vertically on the standing tree. If these fissures display any pronounced irregularities, there is probably a knot or some other blemish lurking inside.

2 *Halve the billets. Set one or two wedges in the center, and drive them to open the billet. Sometimes, a solid blow will split a billet cleanly.*

Riving and preparing the blanks Examine the log for the characteristics mentioned, and if you find that it is worth working, lay a tape measure on it and score the bark at 20 in. and 40 in. Then buck the log into three sections, which are called billets (**1**). One of these 12-in.-diameter billets usually contains just enough wood for two chairs. Halve the billet on the spot using a maul and wedges (**2**).

I use a splitting maul with a short, 22-in.-long handle, which increases my control. You can use a sledge hammer, but the wedge on the maul sometimes comes in handy on a reluctant billet. I also use iron wedges rather than wooden gluts. I split a lot of firewood as well as chair parts, and the iron wedges hold up forever. You should wear safety glasses when striking metal on metal. (You will notice I have forgotten mine in the pictures. Do as I say, not as I do.) Place one wedge on either side of the pith, and work them down in tandem. This placement of wedges helps ensure a straight, even split that bisects the billet. The halves may be small enough to be carried into the shop for riving into turning blanks. If not, quarter them.

3 *Mark the 2-in.-square turning blanks on the end of a section. A wooden maul and a Kent hatchet are ideal for riving pieces of this size.*

You want to obtain as many 2-in.-square blanks as possible from each halved or quartered section. Sketch these out on the end of the sections. I use a splitting hatchet and a wooden maul to rive the blanks (3). A Kent hatchet is best for splitting. It has a wide blade, so it can control a split that extends completely across the end grain of a large section. The head of a Kent hatchet also has a long, gradual taper from the cutting edge to the poll (the surface on which the hatchet is struck). When driven, the thin wedge of the hatchet head bites into the wood and does not bounce back as a fatter wedge is prone to do. A splitting hatchet does not need to be kept as sharp as one that is used for cutting. However, if you want yours to do double duty, keeping it sharpened will not affect its ability to split.

A Kent hatchet has a heavy poll, which can withstand indefinitely the blows of the wooden maul. The maul is a heavy wooden club about 6 in. in diameter and 18 in. long. I turn mine on the lathe from green oak or hickory. A maul has a short life span. It will be gradually knocked apart until it has lost so much weight that it can no longer drive the hatchet with authority. When this happens, I run the old maul through the stove and turn a new one to take its place.

When riving the turning blanks from the sections, it is always best to split pieces of equal mass (4). This does not mean that the outline of the end of the section has to be perfectly bisected. The sections are too irregular. Instead, the amount of surface area should be about equal on either side of the hatchet head, and the resulting two pieces should weigh about the same, even though they may have two very different cross sections. If you do not rive pieces of equal mass, the split will run out toward the side with less mass. Birch is much more susceptible to this run-out than is maple. If a split begins to run out, there is not much you can do to prevent it. However, in addition to legs and stretchers, the chair requires armposts and short spindles that are turned from shorter blanks. Use blanks that have been ruined by run-out for these parts.

4 When riving, always try to place the split so that there is an equal mass of wood on both sides of the hatchet.

Whether you are making a continuous-arm or a sack-back chair, rive enough blanks for four legs and three stretchers. Plan the sequence of splits so that you are always riving blanks of equal mass. Rive 1¼-in.-square blanks for the two armposts and ¾-in.-square blanks for the four short spindles now, too. Next, cut the leg, armpost and short-spindle blanks to the lengths needed for turning. (The distance between the legs determines the lengths of the stretchers, so they are turned after the legs and the sockets in the seat are made. I will discuss the stretchers in Chapter V.) I make my leg blanks 19½ in. long, the armpost blanks 14 in. and the short-spindle blanks 12 in. Each of these lengths includes ½ in. for waste where the blank is attached to the spur drive center of my lathe. Depending on your lathe, you may need to allow more for waste. Each blank also in-

cludes a little extra length so that the through tenons will protrude beyond the sockets, making wedging easier. The rest of the extra length on each leg blank will occur at the foot. This will have to be trimmed after the chair base is assembled for the final time. I like about 1 in. extra on the foot end. That gives me plenty of latitude, so that I do not have to make the seat too low to get all four legs to sit square.

5 *Cut the leg blanks to length. A Swedish brush saw works well for this.*

I cut the blanks to length with a Swedish brush saw (**5**). I like these inexpensive, tubular-metal frame saws because they cut green wood so quickly. Their needle-sharp teeth have a heavy set and cut a wide kerf that does not allow the wet wood to bind on the blade. The blades are inexpensive, and can be resharpened or simply discarded when dull. These saws are available in most hardware stores. I use one with a 21-in. blade.

When all the blanks are the desired length, I remove the high spots and square edges with the drawknife (**6**). It is much easier to do this than turn down the high spots. Long, heavy shavings drawknife off easily; these dry quickly and make excellent kindling.

I generally set the roughly rounded turning blanks aside rather than turn them right away. In as little time as overnight in a heated shop, they will lose a lot of moisture. In the summer, I set them out in the sun for an entire day. Freshly riven wood is so wet that it spits water and does not turn as nicely as it will only 24 hours later.

Turning

Green wood is a joy to turn. Once you have tried it, you will regret any time you have spent in combat with dry, hardwood turning squares. After the green-wood blank is completely round, the chips come off in unbroken lengths like ticker tape, which will pile up on your hands like spaghetti until the tool is obscured and the chips need to be dumped off.

I prefer to turn at the slowest speed possible, which on my lathe is about 1000 rpm. Green wood is soft, and a high rpm is not needed to drive it against the tools. On the other hand, the turning tools need to be kept razor-sharp. The additional pressure needed to make a dull tool cut unseasoned wood will cause the blank to vibrate, which can easily knock the blank out of round because it is so soft. Once it is out of round, the blank is good only for firewood. I cannot place enough stress on the need for razor-sharp lathe tools when turning green wood.

When mounting a dry-wood turning square in the lathe, you can find the center on each end by drawing the diagonals from corner to corner. That is not possible with irregularly shaped, riven turning blanks. I mount them in the lathe by eye. If the blank is obviously off-center and causes the lathe to vibrate dangerously, I will reposition one or both of the ends on the lathe centers. When the blank is centered, turn on the lathe again and watch the blank. The stroboscopic effect of the spinning blank makes the center mass appear solid, and the edges read as a translucent blur. The center mass indicates the largest possible diameter to which the blank can be turned.

6 *Prepare the turning blank for the lathe by removing the high spots and corners with a drawknife.*

I use the baluster leg that is shown on p. 138 for both the continuous-arm and sack-back chairs. My general line consists of these two chairs and a side chair. These are often purchased in sets—two of either armchair and six side chairs. As a result, one leg pattern makes it easier to match the set. I occasionally use the double-bobbin leg, shown on p. 130, for a chair or set of chairs. The double-bobbin leg is simple to turn, so I will describe the turning of a baluster leg here. I will also assume that you are familiar with basic wood-turning techniques.

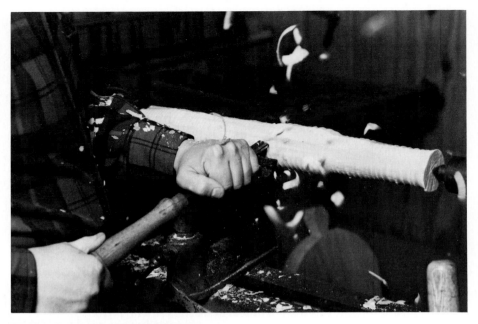

7 *Rough the leg blank to the diameters of the major and minor vases on the leg.*

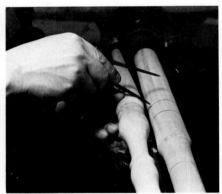

8 *While the blank is spinning, mark the position of the bead and cove above the major vase, and the wafer above the minor vase with a pair of dividers. If you do not have a model leg, determine these points by measuring from a full-scale pattern.*

I do not work from a drawing or template of the baluster leg. Instead, I transfer measurements with calipers directly from a model leg that I have used for years. For your first leg, you will have to work from the drawing on p. 143, or an existing chair. Scale up the drawing to full size and transfer the full-size measurements to the leg blank using calipers. When you have finished your first leg, use it as the model for the remaining legs. Do not worry if all the legs are not identical. When you have made a chair or two, you will probably have produced a leg that seems just right. Keep that leg for your permanent model. I also use a model when turning double-bobbin legs. If I do a special chair that has different legs, I make a model and store it for future reference.

I use only four tools when turning: a ¾-in. gouge, a ¼-in. gouge, a ¾-in. skew and a ½-in. skew. I rough down the blank with the ¾-in. gouge and make the larger shapes with it and the ¾-in. skew. The smaller gouge and skew produce the finer details. I cut with both the gouges and skews, but scrape only with the skews. Scraping must be done carefully with sharp tools, or you will just raise a fuzz. I wear a face shield to protect my face and eyes when I work at the lathe.

First, turn the irregularly shaped blank down to a cylinder with the large gouge (7). The baluster leg has a major and a minor diameter, corresponding to the widest points on the upper and lower vases. (The vases are the two softly rounded swellings on the leg that look just like their namesake.) Set two pairs of calipers to these diameters on the model leg or full-scale drawing, and rough the blank to those diameters, checking with the calipers. The minor diameter, at the top of the leg, extends about two-fifths the length of the blank. It is best worked on the end of the blank that is fixed to the tailstock center. The foot is fixed to the drive center. The waste attached to the drive center will be trimmed off later when the leg is cut to length.

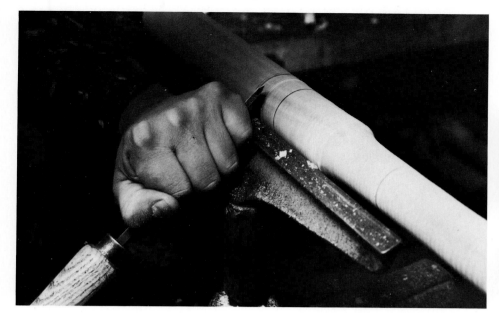

9 Cut the sides of a bead with a skew (left), then round it by scraping.

10 Cut the cove with a small gouge, working down to the bottom from both sides (left). Use a skew to clean the fillet between the cove and the bead with a scraping cut (right).

Next, locate the three points *A, B* and *C* shown on the leg pattern in Chapter XII. I do this by holding the model leg parallel to the spinning blank. Line up the end of the tenon with the tailstock end of the blank. If the lengths of the legs vary, I want the variation to occur at the foot of each, where any extra length can be trimmed off without affecting the tenon. (If you are setting out the leg from a pattern drawing, start at the tenon end.) Lightly scribe each point by laying one leg of a sharp pair of dividers on the model and touching the point of the leg to the spinning blank (**8**). I complete the turning by eye, having done it thousands of times before. You will probably want to work more slowly and compare the turning to the model or pattern more often.

Scribe marks *A* and *B* indicate the bead and cove that separate the tapered foot from the major vase. The bead takes up about two fifths of the distance between these two lines. The remaining three fifths are needed for the cove. I eyeball this division. I make the bead with a skew, pushing in on each side with the tool cutting, not scraping (**9**). Round the bead by scraping gently with the skew.

Make the cove with a small gouge (**10**). Cut (don't scrape) from both sides down to the lowest point. Allow room for the fillet that divides the bead and cove. The fillet makes the transition from the convex to the concave shape sharp and distinct. As you deepen the cove, you will expose end grain on its sides. If one of the cuts should move beyond the lowest point, the gouge will grab in the end grain, and will be sent spiraling up the leg. This will usually ruin the turning. Once the cove is made, clean the fillet with the heel or toe of a skew.

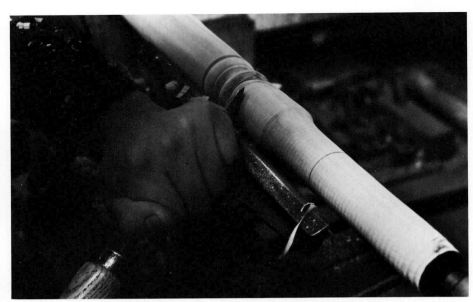

11 *Form the bottom of the major vase with the heel of the skew. Remember to allow for the wafer beneath the cove.*

12 *Reduce the wafer's diameter by cutting gently with the skew (top). Then cut the wafer's radius with the skew's heel.*

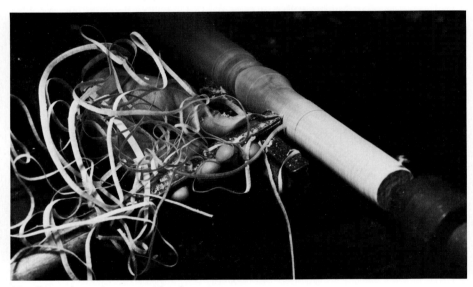

13 *Shape the major vase with a large gouge.*

Next, shape the bottom of the major vase and the sharp, waferlike ring that divides the vase from the cove. Allowing room for the wafer, start the vase by making successive angled cuts with the heel of the large skew (**11**). The vase should have a round bottom, so be careful that your cuts produce a curved profile, not a straight one.

Reduce the diameter of the wafer with the skew (**12**). If you leave the wafer the same diameter as the major vase and the bead, it will be more exposed and in greater danger of being damaged. One side of the wafer is formed by a side of the cove. Cut the other side to a radius with a skew, making the edge of the wafer sharp.

Move up the blank and shape the rest of the major vase. I do this with the ¾-in. gouge (**13**). Cut the neck of the vase so that it will be thinner than the largest diameter of the minor vase, as shown on the pattern drawing. The neck slopes and finishes with a cove. When shaping the neck, you will have reduced considerably the diameter of the blank, and it may vibrate or buzz under the pressure of the tool. You can eliminate this vibration by using one hand as a steady rest. Hook the handle of the tool under your right elbow, pinching it against your ribs. Grip the turning tool with your right hand close to the tool's cutting edge and lock your wrist. Control the tool by turning your torso. Sup-

port the turning from behind with your left hand. Do not push too hard with the left hand; push just enough to duplicate the pressure of the tool on the other side of the turning. Keep your palm open. You do not want to catch your skin between the spinning wood and the tool rest. I have sufficient calluses on my left hand so that the heat caused by the friction does not bother me. If it is uncomfortable for you, wear a thin glove.

Cut the cove that ends the major vase with the small gouge (**14**). Cut the right-angled stop that separates the cove from the neck with a skew. This stop should be good and sharp, without any raggedness at the transition.

14 *Use a small gouge to cut the cove that ends the major vase (bottom). Make the cove's stop with a small skew; use your free hand to control vibration (top).*

15 *Shape the bottom of the minor vase and its wafer with a skew.*

Move to the right of the cove and cut the bottom of the minor vase with a skew. This cut should form a radius, to give the vase a round bottom. A wafer separates the bottom of the minor vase from the cove. Reduce it in diameter and round it to a sharp edge with a skew, as was done for the wafer under the major vase (**15**).

Now move to the other end of the blank and shape the tapered foot. I am always careful in making any turning to do the center first, then work in both directions away from the center to the ends. This is contrary to the natural tendency of a right-handed person to begin at the left-hand end of a turning and work along the blank to the other end. If you cut one or both of the ends before the middle, however, you weaken the blank considerably and increase the amount it will vibrate on the lathe.

I have noticed a tendency of a tapered cone to appear to have a convex, slightly bulging profile, sort of like a carrot. To compensate for this tendency, I make the taper just slightly concave along its length. The classical Greeks made their temple columns slightly convex along their length to compensate for the tendency of a straight column to appear concave. This convexity is called entasis. Perhaps the slight concavity of the leg taper could be called reverse entasis.

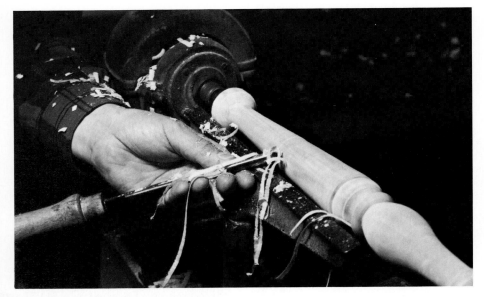

16 *Make the tapered foot with a large gouge (top). Complete the end of the foot with a large skew.*

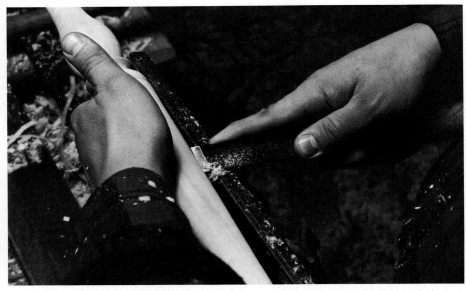

17 *Clean up the taper with a planing cut. Only one edge of the skew should touch the rest.*

Shape the taper with the large gouge (**16**). When the shape is completely developed, clean up the last 1 in. or so of the foot with a skew. I do this by holding the large skew with its wide side flat on the rest, as I would if I were about to scrape. I raise the cutting edge slightly above center and feed the skew straight into the wood. This leaves a wafer of waste on the end that can be knocked off later with a drawknife.

Next, clean up any gouge marks on the tapered foot. I do this with the ¾-in. skew as well. Start at the top, or right-hand end of the taper, just below the bead. Lay the wide side of the skew on the rest as when cleaning up the foot. I lift the right edge of the skew so that it is rotated about 45°. In this position, the skew is in contact with the rest only on one corner of its left edge. Support the turning with your left hand to prevent it from vibrating, and slowly move the skew along the taper (**17**). The chip cuts loose in more of a clump than the ribbon that you usually obtain when cutting. The surface is cut perfectly clean, and should require no sanding.

I call this a planing cut. It is a difficult technique to refine. But once it is mastered, you will be able to use the skew for cleaning up any straight surfaces, as on the taper or any gradually concave or convex surfaces. I use this planing cut on the bobbins of the stretchers, on the entire double-bobbin leg and on the taper and vase of the baluster leg and armpost.

Before leaving the tapered foot, scribe a ring on it to locate the stretcher socket. Set a dividers from the model leg or pattern by placing one leg on the scribe line and the other at the point where the bead meets the taper. Place the dividers in the same position on the spinning blank and push the leg into the taper to scribe the ring (**18**).

18 *Scribe a ring on the tapered foot to locate the stretcher socket.*

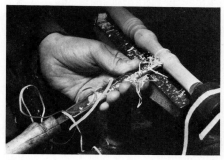

19 *Turn the neck of the minor vase and the tapered tenon with a large gouge. Form a slight swelling where the neck meets the tenon.*

20 *The armpost is a miniature leg, and the same techniques are used to turn it. The tapered tenon on the lower end of the armpost is the same size as the tenon for the legs. The tenon at its upper end fits into a 7/16-in.-tapered socket.*

Slide the tool rest to the other end of the blank to shape the last details there. Relieve the neck of the minor vase with the large gouge. I turn a slight swelling on the neck where it meets the tenon.

This swelling allows the diameter of the vase's neck to be less than that of the base of the tapered tenon. The swelling looks something like a shoulder, but it has no mechanical function. The point at which the leg disappears under the edge of the seat occurs along the neck of the vase. It appears to the viewer that the leg continues to taper down to a very small diameter. Actually, the vase swells to form a strong, robust tenon. The swelling contributes to the illusion of delicacy that is also seen in the shaping of the seat.

Shape the tapered tenon with the large gouge (**19**). I determine the amount of taper by eye, but you may want to make a gauge. Bore a 5/8-in. hole in a piece of 2-in.-thick pine scrap. Ream this hole with a tapered reamer, as described in Chapter IV. To use the gauge, you will have to remove the leg from the lathe. To recenter the leg perfectly after gauging the tenon, you must relocate the end on the drive center exactly as it was. This can be difficult to do. I grind a small notch in the beveled edge of one of the spurs on the drive center. This notch creates a dimple in one of the marks left by the spurs in the end grain of the turning. Aligning the dimpled mark with the notched spur should recenter the leg perfectly.

If you are using a straight tenon on the leg, measure its diameter with a pair of calipers. Set the calipers from the bit you will use to bore the seat sockets, rather than setting it with a ruler. This prevents mistakes in measuring. The swelling at the top of the neck decreases suddenly in diameter to form the tenon's shoulder.

The two armposts are turned in the same sequence and manner as the legs (**20**). I turn tapered tenons at both ends. The tenon on the lower end is the same size as that on the legs, and it can be tested using the same gauge. You can make another gauge for the upper tenon, which fits into the arm. Bore a 7/16-in. hole in a piece of 1/2-in. scrap and taper the hole with the reamer.

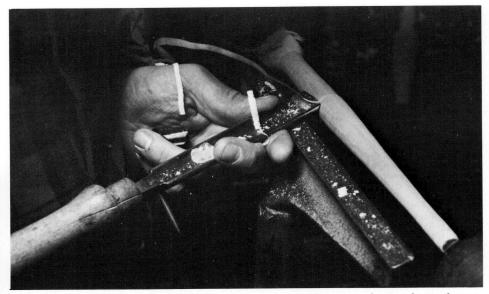

21 *Shape the short spindles with a large gouge to a continuous sweep from end to end.*

22 *The neck forms the top tenon; check its diameter with a pair of calipers.*

Both the sack-back and the continuous-arm chairs have two short spindles behind each armpost. These spindles are also turned. They are at the limit of the ratio of length to thickness that can be turned without intolerable vibration. Be careful when turning them and use your hand as a steady rest. Turn the spindle blanks to shape with the large gouge (**21**). The outline is a clean, continuous sweep from the shoulder of the lower tenon up over a gentle swelling and down to a ⁷⁄₁₆-in. neck (**22**). The neck also forms the upper tenon. To

achieve a smooth outline, make a final clean-up pass, planing gently with a sharp skew (**23**). This finishing technique is only mastered with considerable practice. If it is too difficult at first, let the spindle dry, then sand the surface smooth. Be sure to sand in the direction of the grain.

Rather than spending time trying to make the lower, shouldered tenon a perfect fit for a ⁹⁄₁₆-in. socket, I turn the tenon slightly egg-shaped and oversized (**24**). Next to the shoulder, I make the neck a little narrower than the bit that will be used to bore the socket. When I assemble the chair, I can shave the egg with a chisel to fit perfectly in the socket. Also, the chisel produces a faceted surface that bites into the soft-pine walls of the socket. These facets help resist torque that might otherwise weaken the joint.

23 *Clean up the surface with a planing cut of the skew chisel.*

24 *Use a small gouge and skew to make the lower, egg-shaped tenon. The neck below the tenon's shoulder should be a little narrower than the socket, and the egg should be a little wider.*

I never sand turnings on the lathe. Green wood does not sand well. And on any wood, green or dry, sanding on the spinning lathe will create concentric scratches that are almost impossible to remove, no matter how fine the paper. Also, sanding softens the crisp details that I have taken so much care to make. Good control of sharp tools will eliminate the need for almost all sanding. Between turning and assembly, the parts will have been bumped and will have had glue spilled on them. Some grain will rise as the parts dry. There-fore, I find it most efficient to sand with 220-grit paper after the chair is assembled, just before applying the first coat of paint. Anything I miss will be abraded away by steel wool when I smooth the first coat of paint.

Chapter IV

Socketing the Seat

You have completed the seat, the legs, the two armposts and the short spindles. Before the stretchers can be turned, the sockets for the legs must be bored in the seat. The legs and sockets are angled to the seat, and it is worthwhile to take a look at why this is so.

Vertical legs are ideal for supporting downward pressure. However, we do not use chairs in an ideal manner. We do not sit bolt upright like West Point cadets at mealtime. We recline and shift and squirm. These forces are transmitted throughout the chair in other directions than just downward. For example, as we shift in the chair to find a comfortable position, we create torque, a twisting motion of the seat against the legs. The same force is exerted in a wrestling match. A wrestler does not throw his opponent by pushing downward on his shoulders. He does so by wrenching him sideways. To resist this wrenching torque, the other wrestler braces himself by spreading his legs and arms apart and throwing his shoulders forward. His legs and arms are now splayed in two planes very much like those of a Windsor.

It may seem strange to compare a chair and sitter to a pair of wrestlers, but the relationship often seems no less adversarial. When we approach a chair, we turn and flop ourselves into it. The chair is suddenly and violently stressed by the 100 lb. to 200 lb. of humanity landing in it. We then twist and turn until we have found a comfortable position. This strains the legs and the stretcher system as well as the back. We shift our weight by sliding our buttocks forward or backward, or by crossing and uncrossing our legs. When we stretch, we prop our shoulders against the chair back and our bottoms against the front of the seat. In spite of mother's warnings, we still rock back on the legs. When we finally get out of the chair, we put yet another strain on it. Instead of lifting our own weight with our legs, we put our hands on the arms of the chair and push ourselves up.

To better resist these assaults, each leg of a Windsor is canted in two planes, away from both its adjacent partners. This widens the base of the chair (the points formed by the intersection of the legs with the floor). This wider base makes a chair resistant to the stresses and strains put upon it. It also makes the chair less likely to roll out from underneath the sitter, should he lean too far forward, backward or to the side.

To discuss the specific leg-to-seat angles, it is necessary to define two terms—splay and rake. In normal use, both words mean the same thing, but I define them differently for Windsors. Splay refers to the way that the two front legs (and the two rear legs) are canted away from each other. When looking at a chair from the front or back, you see the splay of the legs. Rake refers to the way that the two legs on a single side are canted away from each other. Rake is seen by regarding the chair from either side.

Splay and rake combine to resist the compression and torque caused by the sitter's movements and to stabilize and prevent the chair from tipping. However, it is possible to have too much of a good thing, and a chair is weakened if the legs are splayed or raked excessively. I consider between 105° and 110° to be a good splay for front and back legs. A chair is weakened if these angles exceed about 113°. Also, front legs that are splayed too much continually get in the way: They make it difficult to get in and out of the chair, and people passing by the chair trip over them. Other chairs cannot be placed close to a chair with excessively splayed legs, which makes such a chair awkward to have around a table.

It is not necessary to splay the rear legs to the same angles as the front legs. However, if they are not splayed enough, or are placed too close together, they cease to stabilize the chair. In the extreme, rear legs placed too upright act as a single point, and the chair becomes like a three-legged stool. When a chair with upright rear legs is rocked back, there is little to prevent it from rolling sideways.

Rear legs should have a distinct rake, because the majority of the sitter's weight will be supported by these legs. The backs of all Windsors recline; those designed for relaxing or reading have a more distinct recline. The greater the slope of the back, the farther the sitter's weight is carried backward. If the rake of the back legs is insufficient, the chair has a precarious balance when in use. The rake should increase with the slope of the back. I am most comfortable with a chair whose back legs are raked about 110° to 113° degrees. A rake of less than 107° is insufficient.

This much rake is unnecessary for the front legs, because there is relatively less weight placed over them. When the sitter leans forward, he has his own legs under him for additional support; when he leans back, he has only the chair. Raking the front legs as much as the rear would only encumber people walking by the chair or make it more difficult for the sitter to get out of it. Too much rake, like too much splay, can also weaken the chair. However, no rake at all is dangerous. When the sitter leans forward on front legs with no rake, the chair pivots on the legs, and it can kick out backward from underneath its occupant. I prefer a rake of about 95° to 100° for the front legs.

1 *Spoon bits are ideal for Windsor chairmaking. The semicircular end is sharpened, and does all the cutting.*

Before boring the sockets, you should know about spoon bits. You are not uninformed if you do not know what these bits are. They were dropped from toolmaker's product lines early in this century, and were considered obsolete until the recent revival of interest in making furniture by hand. Spoon bits are one of the most ancient tools. They were known to the Romans and have been excavated from Viking sites. By the eighteenth century, they were known as chair bits.

Spoon bits have a number of properties that make them ideal for chairmaking: The speed of cut can be regulated, the angle of a socket can be altered as you bore, and sockets can be bored at very shallow angles to the work.

To understand a spoon bit and how it works, imagine a test tube sliced in half along its length. Each half would closely resemble a spoon bit. The semicircular end of the tool is the business end and does all the cutting (**1**). If the end is pushed into the surface of a piece of

wood, it will score a half-round line similar to what could be made by a carving gouge. Unlike the cutting edge of a gouge, however, the upturned nose of the spoon will also undercut. As the bit is turned by the brace, this scoring becomes a complete circle. If only one turn is made, a little round undercut plug can be popped loose.

You may have guessed from the comparison with a gouge that pressure is what makes the spoon bit cut. The more weight placed behind the bit, the deeper its nose will score. The chairmaker's weight on the brace provides the pressure. There is no lead screw on a spoon bit to regulate the speed of the cut—you have total control. By controlling the amount of weight on the brace, you can easily regulate the speed. You can bore a ⅝-in. socket in a 1½-in.-thick birch leg with only 15 to 20 turns of the brace. By applying less weight, you can cut as slowly as desired. This is very useful when boring sockets in slender parts, such as bows and arms.

Without a lead screw, the round nose of a spoon allows the user to alter the angle of the socket even after it is half-way completed. When assembling chairs by eye, this ability to adjust the angle after you have begun to bore the socket is essential. It is also possible when using a spoon bit to bore sockets whose angles are as shallow as 30°, such as where the outermost long spindles meet the bow of the sack back and the arm of the continuous arm.

Spoon bits are seldom perfectly symmetrical, so they will wobble slightly when turned. This is not a problem when using a hand brace, but you must never use a spoon bit in a drill press or an electric drill.

2 *Mark the positions of the seat sockets through holes punched in the pattern.*

3 *Place a backing board beneath the seat, so that you do not bore into the benchtop.*

Boring the Sockets

Now that you have been introduced to splay and rake and the spoon bit, you are ready to bore the sockets. The procedure is the same for both seats, so I will demonstrate using the shield seat. First, position the seat pattern on the top of the seat and transfer the locations of the leg sockets as well as those for the armposts and the short and long spindles. I mark them by pressing a pencil point through small holes that have been made at the proper locations (2). I am not a slave to the pattern. It merely gives me an idea of where the sockets should be. The seats are hand-made, so they will not be exactly perfect in either shape or outline. If the seat is not precisely symmetrical, for example, some adjustments may be required in the placement of some or all of the sockets to balance their positions on the seat.

When you are satisfied with the socket placements, fasten the seat to the bench with the hold-down frame or hand-screw clamps. Put a backing piece under the seat so that you do not bore into the bench when the bit exits the bottom of the seat (3). If you use clamps, place the seat on a corner of the bench so that you have access to it from the front and both sides.

The sockets are ⅝ in. in diameter, and are bored from the top of the seat. Boring them from below would ruin the top surface when the bit breaks through. Clamping a waste block to the top of the seat to prevent break-out would be difficult, if not impossible, because of the contour of the surface. It would be equally difficult to bore the holes from the bottom before shaping the seat. Imagine trying to work a concave surface that has four holes in it. Every time the tool ran into one of these, it would dive, creating a depression around the hole.

Before making the first socket, it is not a bad idea to practice using the spoon bit. When using a spoon bit, always start the socket by holding the brace and bit at a right angle to the work. To prevent the nose from wandering, gently push it into the wood's surface. Now turn slowly. The first couple of turns will produce a distinct, volute shaving. The scored circumference will quickly increase to the bit's diameter. A full-width, unbroken shaving will begin to rise up the hollow shaft of the spoon, like a cork being withdrawn from a bottle. After the nose is buried in the wood, the brace can be gradually pulled to the desired angle. Be sure to keep turning the bit as you maneuver it into position.

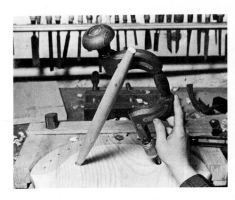

4 *You can use an adjustable bevel square to determine the splay (shown here) and rake angles while boring the sockets. Sight along the axis of the brace and bit to the blade of the bevel square and adjust accordingly.*

5 *Establish the rake and splay angles of the second socket with a dummy leg inserted in the first socket. The axes of the dummy leg and the brace and bit should intersect to form an isosceles triangle. Notice how the intersections differ for the shield seat (top) and the oval seat (bottom)—yet both form isosceles triangles.*

If you do not own spoon bits, I am at a loss to recommend other types that will work satisfactorily, because I have not used most of them. I know that an auger bit will tear out when boring a hole at an angle because the spurs cannot score a complete circle. I suggest that you experiment with bits that you own to see if they will work.

To bore the first socket in the seat, you will need to establish the rake and splay angles for it. I use measurements and angles from model chairs that we use in our kitchen—when they are not in the shop. (After all these years, my wife still does not have either a complete or a matching set of chairs.) I work by eye, referring to the model chair before boring. I have done this so often that I have a feel for the correct angles. For your first chair, however, you might feel a little bit more secure with some assistance from a protractor or an adjustable bevel square. I will describe and show how to use bevel squares. If you are not copying an existing chair, take the angles from the drawings on pp. 131 and 139.

It does not matter which leg socket is bored first. Out of habit, I generally start with the left rear. The first socket is easy because it need not duplicate angles already existing in the seat. But this is a mixed blessing because an existing angle could be used for reference. So, when boring the first socket, you're on your own. You need be concerned only that its angles are reasonably close to the same splay and rake as the plan drawings, the model or the rest of the chairs in a set.

A chair is not generally viewed from the rear, so the tolerances for splay and rake are greater here than for the front legs. Set the blade of the bevel square to the splay angle and place its stock on the flat surface at the back of the seat. Establish the rake by eye or set another bevel square or protractor from the drawings or a model chair. Although you cannot measure the bit directly against the angled blades, you can sight along the bit to each blade to estimate the desired angle.

Start the socket with the bit vertical. As you turn the brace, gradually pull it down to the final angles. Refer to the bevel squares as you make this adjustment (4). You can gain a better vantage for judging the splay by squatting down in front of the seat, still holding the top of the brace. When the angles are right, bore about halfway through the seat. Then stop and check the splay and rake against the bevel squares. Correct if necessary and finish boring the socket.

The completed socket supplies a reference for establishing the splay and rake of the second rear leg. For this reference, I use a dummy leg, which is no more than a dowel with a shouldered tenon turned to the same diameter as the spoon bit for the socket. I keep four of these dummy legs on hand. Insert a dummy leg into the first socket, from the top of the seat. To bore the second socket at the correct splay and rake angles, the brace and bit need to mirror the position of the dummy leg. (The axis of the brace and bit forms an isosceles triangle with the axis of the dummy leg and the bottom of the seat. You

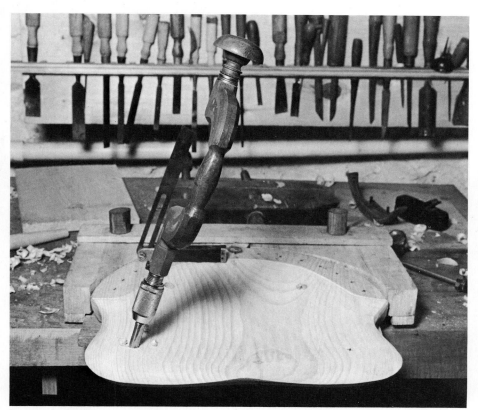

6 *Gauge the splay of the front leg against a bevel square. You can estimate the shallow rake of the leg.*

7 *Use a dummy leg to find the rake and splay angles of the second front-leg socket.*

will remember from high-school geometry that this triangle has identical base angles.) Start the second socket vertically. As you turn the bit, move the brace into position to complete the isosceles triangle (5).

When you are happy with the splay adjustment, pull the brace toward the front of the seat until the axes of the brace and bit and the dummy leg create an imaginary plane. This plane establishes the rake. These relationships—the identical base angles and the two axes in the same plane—geometrically produce both rake and splay angles for the second rear-leg socket.

When the brace is finally in position, remove the dummy leg and start to bore. About halfway through, stop and verify the setting of the brace to make sure it has not wandered. Do this by reinserting the dummy leg and squatting again in front of the seat to view the triangle. Also check that the axes are still in the same plane. Adjust the angles of the brace and bit if necessary and complete the socket.

The first front-leg socket poses the same problems as the first rear-leg socket. Again, the splay can be gauged by sighting along the brace and bit to a bevel square resting on the flat back of the seat (6). If the front of the seat overhangs the bench, you will have to make an educated guess as to the rake. There is no way to put a gauge in line behind the brace. The angle of rake for a front leg is not easily noticed by an observer because a chair is usually viewed from the front, and rake is only visible from the side. In addition, the rake is quite small—the leg is very near perpendicular. These two factors allow for a considerable margin of error.

Begin the socket and establish the angles. Bore about halfway through, check for accuracy, then complete the socket. The second front-leg socket is bored just like the second rear-leg socket, using a dummy leg to establish an imaginary isosceles triangle and plane with the brace and bit (7).

8 *Gauge the flare and slope angles of the armposts against a bevel square. Here the bevel is set for the slope angle.*

Armpost sockets The armposts are also set at two angles to the seat. They lean forward and outward. I use two more terms to define these angles. The spindles and armposts radiate away from each other like the fingers on an open hand. I call this outward lean "flare." These parts also lean either toward the front or the back of the seat, and I call this "slope." Therefore, the armposts flare outward from each other and slope forward.

The armpost sockets are also ⅝ in. in diameter, and the procedure for boring them is the same as that for the leg sockets. Begin by starting the hole with the spoon bit held at a right angle to the seat. Once the nose of the bit is set, hold a bevel square against the bit to establish the flare. Then, as you turn the brace, pull it forward and measure it against another bevel square set for slope (**8**). When you are sure of the angles, bore halfway through the seat, check the angles again, make corrections, then finish the socket.

Insert one of the dummy legs into the socket, then stand back and take a look at the seat. The armposts flare outward, so they cannot form an isosceles triangle with the seat as base. I establish the angles of the second armpost by eye, placing the brace so that its axis is a mirror image of the dummy leg (**9**). If you do not trust your eye, you can always rely on bevel squares. Start the hole and then bring the brace into the flare position. Use the plane formed by the axes of the dowel and brace to find the forward slope. Bore about halfway through, check the angles, then complete the hole. (I bore the sockets for the spindles now. A beginner should probably do this after assembling the seat, legs and stretchers, so I will discuss these sockets in Chapter VIII.)

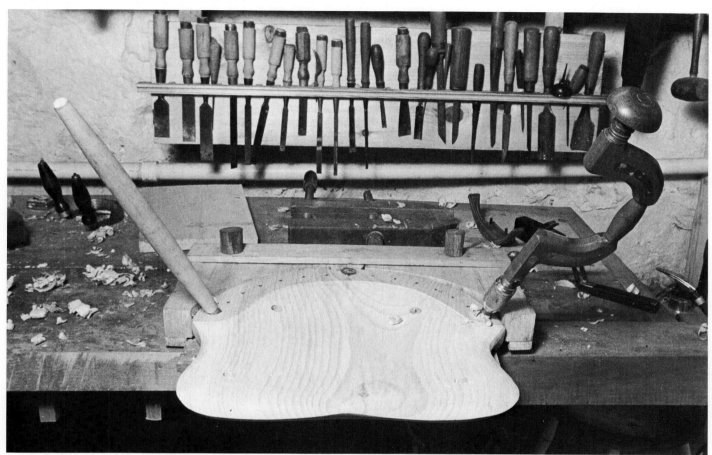

9 *Establish the flare and slope angles of the second armpost socket by eye, positioning the brace and bit to mirror a dummy leg inserted in the first armpost socket.*

Before removing the seat from the bench, insert another dummy leg into the second armpost socket. Back away from the seat and squat down to judge the angles. If there is a discrepancy, make a mental note of it so you can correct it later with the tapered reamer.

Unclamp the seat, insert all four dummy legs and set them upright on the benchtop to check the accuracy of the four leg sockets. Mark on the bottom of the seat or make a mental note of any that are out of line for correction with the reamer.

11 *When reaming the second socket of a front or back pair, the brace and reamer should mirror a leg inserted in the already reamed socket. A bevel square can help check the splay.*

10 *The sockets must be reamed to take the tapered tenons. The socket angles can be corrected at the same time. Here the splay is checked against a bevel square.*

12 *Taper the armpost sockets with the reamer. The flare and slope angles can be corrected by gauging each armpost against the other, and against a bevel square.*

Tapering the Sockets

If you are using simple through tenons, no more need be done to the sockets. For tapered joints, however, the sockets still need to be reamed. The reamer, as mentioned earlier, resembles a steel cone that has been sliced in half along its axis. It is a scraping tool, so the two beveled edges can be sharpened with a file and honed with a medium-grit stone. The bevels should be flat, and you must be sure not to round them or to turn a burr on them. Either will prevent the reamer from cutting.

Remove the dummy legs from the seat and clamp it on edge in a bench vise, with the bottom facing out toward the work area. Secure the tapered reamer in the chuck of a brace and insert the reamer's business end into one of the sockets. As you turn the brace, feed the reamer slowly into the socket. If you feed the reamer too quickly, it will ride over the end grain and make the socket oval. Let the tool scrape its way into the socket. You cannot speed up the action by applying pressure to the reamer. The harder the wood you are working, the more time required to ream the sockets.

Use the reamer to make adjustments in the angles of the sockets. For example, if a front leg has insufficient splay, you can increase the angle by pulling the brace out toward the seat edge as you ream the hole. Set an adjustable bevel square to indicate how much correction is needed (**10**).

13 *The chair takes shape.*

Crank the brace and feed the reamer until you think the socket has been opened enough to receive its leg tenon. The entire tapered tenon, but no more, should fit into the socket. Some of the tenon should protrude above the seat to make wedging easier. Test by inserting the tenon into the socket, and ream further if necessary. I have turned so many legs that the tenons are all nearly identical. Yours may not be. Therefore, it would be best if you fitted each tenon to a particular socket and marked the matching pairs. As you continue to make chairs, you will eventually be able to skip this step.

Ream all the leg sockets. The angles of the second front or rear socket to be reamed can be judged against a leg inserted in the first reamed socket. A bevel square will also help (**11**). Reverse the seat and ream the armpost sockets, correcting the slope and flare angles if necessary (**12**). The armposts and sockets should also be test-fitted and marked in pairs. The armpost tenons should protrude beneath the seat so they can be wedged at assembly.

When all the sockets have been bored and reamed, you can insert the legs and armposts into the seat and see the chair taking shape (**13**).

Chapter V

Turning the Stretchers and Assembling the Undercarriage

In this chapter, I will describe how to measure and make the stretchers, bore the sockets for the stretcher tenons, and assemble the legs, stretchers and seat. The procedure is exactly the same for both the sack-back and continuous-arm chairs, and is the same whether you use baluster or double-bobbin turnings, locking tapered tenons for the legs or straight through tenons. I will use the sack back as an example.

The chair is handmade, so the distances between the legs will vary slightly. For this reason, it is best to figure the lengths of the stretchers from the particular chair you are making, rather than from a drawing. I will discuss the side stretchers, the ones that extend between the front and back legs, first.

Side Stretchers

Insert the leg tenons into the seat sockets; I usually tap the foot of each leg with a hammer to make the joint self-lock. Set the chair upright on a bench to measure the stretcher lengths. First measure the inside dimension between a pair of front and back legs, at the height of the scribe marks on the tapered feet (**1**). This measurement for my sack-back Windsor is usually between 11½ in. and 12½ in.

You will remember that the stretchers are meant to push the legs apart, not hold them together. To ensure that this critical tension is created, I add ¼ in. to the distance between the front and back legs. You must also add the lengths of the stretcher's two tenons. I turn my Windsor legs to a diameter of 1½ in. at the scribe marks, so I make each stretcher tenon 1¼ in. long.

Thus, the total length of a side stretcher is the sum of the following: the inside distance between the front and back legs, ¼ in. for the extra spread, and the combined lengths of the stretcher's two tenons. For one of my sack backs, the length of one side stretcher might be:

$$11\frac{1}{2} + \frac{1}{4} + 2\frac{1}{2} = 14\frac{1}{4}$$

When I trim the turning blank to length, I also include ½ in. for waste at the drive-center end of the turning. You may want to add more for waste, depending on your lathe.

If you have been careful, the front and back legs on each side of the chair will be the same distance apart, and the stretchers will be the same length. It is possible that one stretcher will have to be longer than the other—measure to check and, after turning the stretchers, mark them to avoid confusion.

1 Insert the legs and measure the distance between each pair of front and back legs.

2 Turn the side-stretcher blank down to a 1½-in.-diameter cylinder.

3 To mark the center of a side-stretcher, set a dividers at one-half the stretcher's visible length. Place the right leg a tenon length from the blank's tailstock end and push the left leg into the spinning wood.

Turning The blanks for the stretchers were rived at the same time as the leg blanks (p. 33). Trim them to length, as described on the facing page, then remove their corners with a drawknife. Secure one of the side-stretcher blanks in the lathe, and turn it down to a 1½-in. diameter cylinder—the largest diameter of the finished stretcher (**2**). I use a ¾-in. gouge for this. I take this diameter directly from my model chair with calipers. (Drawings for the stretchers are shown in Chapters XI and XII.)

To lay out the stretcher, set a dividers to one-half the visible length of the side stretcher. The visible length is the inside distance between the legs plus ¼ in. For the stretcher we've calculated, the visible length is 11¾ in., so the dividers would be set at 5⅞ in. (Remember to calculate from your own chair.) Measure the length of a tenon in from the tailstock end of the blank. Turn on the lathe, and lay the right leg of the dividers against the wood at this point. Push the point of the left leg into the spinning blank (**3**). The scribed mark locates the center of the stretcher. Later, you will use the mark to locate the socket for the center stretcher.

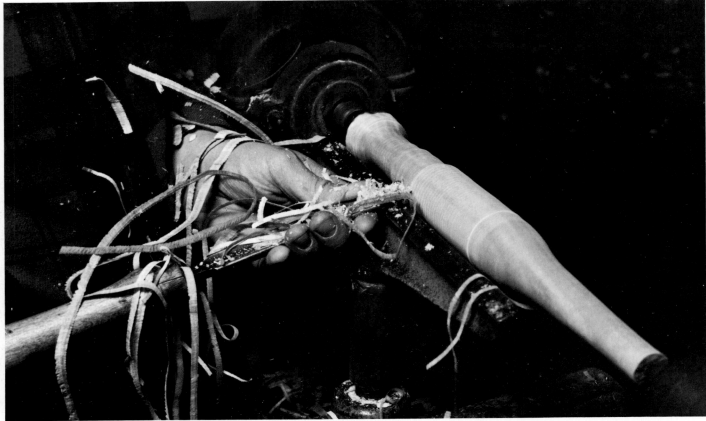

4 *Rough-out the bobbin-shaped stretcher with a large gouge. Start from the ends and work in toward the middle to form the swelling.*

Rough-out the simple bobbin shape of the stretcher. The techniques are similar to those described for turning the major vase on the baluster leg. Start several inches from one end and make a single pass, cutting out to that end. Begin the next pass about ½ in. closer to the center of the blank (**4**). Repeating this process a number of times reduces the diameter of the end of the stretcher and automatically starts the development of the bobbin.

With practice, you will learn to make the cuts of a certain length and thickness so that the swelling for the bobbin occurs right where you want it. Rough-out the last 1¼ in. of the blank to about ¾ in. in diameter for the tenon. Move the tool rest and rough-out the other half of the stretcher in the same way.

Next, place one leg of the dividers (still set to one-half the stretcher's visible length) on the center scribe mark. Reach out with the free leg and scribe the shoulders of the tenons on each end of the blank (**5**). I make the tenons egg-shaped so that the wet sockets will shrink around them and form locking rings, as described in Chapter II. The thickness of the tenon should slightly exceed that of the socket. If the tenons fit perfectly now, they will be undersized when dried in hot sand before assembly. I bore all the sockets in the un-

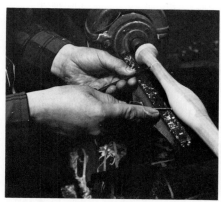

5 *Scribe a mark for the tenon shoulder with a pair of dividers.*

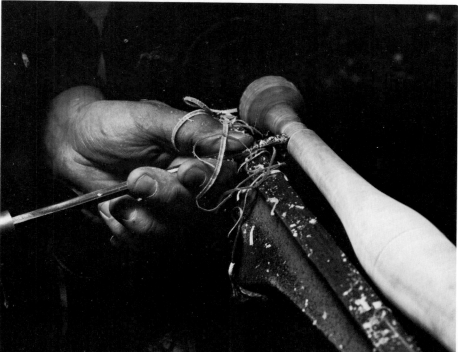

6 *Turn the tenon ¾ in. in diameter (top right), then make it egg-shaped by cutting two grooves with a small gouge.*

7 *Finish the profile by making a planing cut with a skew chisel.*

dercarriage using the same ⅝-in. spoon bit used for the leg and armpost sockets in the seat. Therefore, I finish the tenons of the side stretchers to no more than ¾ in. in diameter.

When the tenon is the correct diameter, make two rings in it with a small turning gouge (**6**). The first ring should be right next to the shoulder so that the tenon now has a distinct neck. The second is made about halfway down the length of the tenon. I round the end of each tenon with a ½-in. skew. This makes the tenon end conform to the round bottom of the socket. Also, the joint will fit tightly and require a lot of pressure to assemble. The rounded ends will not get hung up on the walls of the socket during assembly.

Make a planing cut with the ¾-in. skew over the entire profile to clean it up (**7**). When the stretcher is complete, remove it from the lathe and trim the waste from the drive-center end. Turn the other side stretcher in the same way. Remember, if the legs are not the same distance apart, the two side stretchers will vary in length. If so, mark the stretchers to avoid confusion.

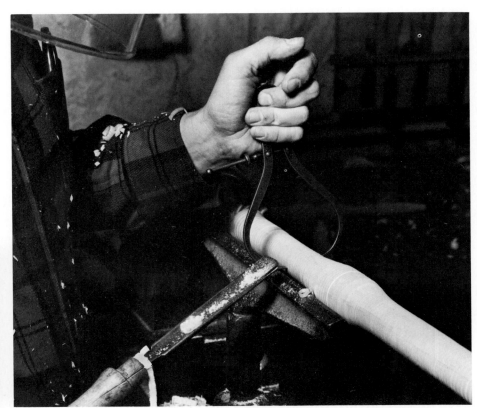

8 *Find the center of the stretcher, then turn the blank on either side of the bobbin down to the diameter of the arrow-shaped turnings.*

Center Stretcher

It is easy to calculate the lengths of the side stretchers because the distance between the legs can be measured directly. It is not possible to measure for the center stretcher directly because I turn all three stretchers before boring the sockets and assembling the chair. I determine its length in two steps.

The first step is to calculate the length of the center stretcher, excluding the tenons. This is the visible length of the stretcher (L), and it can be found with the formula:

$$\left(\frac{x + y}{2} - d\right) + \tfrac{1}{4} = L$$

In the formula, x is the measured center-to-center distance between the front legs at the height of the scribe; y is the measured center-to-center distance between the rear legs at the height of the scribe. (It is easy to get the center-to-

center distance by measuring from the inside of one leg to the outside of its mate.) Dividing the sum of these measurements by 2 gives the center-to-center length at the position of the stretcher, midway between the front and back legs. Subtracting two radii of the side stretchers at their scribe marks gives the visible length of the center stretcher. Two radii equals one diameter—d in the equation—so I simply measure with calipers the thickness of one side stretcher at the scribe mark. The extra ¼ in. ensures that the center stretcher also pushes the legs apart.

The center-to-center distance between the front legs of my sack-back chair usually measures between 16½ in. and 17¾ in. Let's take a 17-in. measurement for example, so $x = 17$ in. For the rear legs, let's call the center-to-center distance (y) 14½ in. The diameter of the side stretchers at the scribe mark (d) is 1½ in. So the visible length of the center stretcher is 14½ in.:

$$\left(\frac{17 + 14\frac{1}{2}}{2} - 1\frac{1}{2}\right) + \tfrac{1}{4} = 14\frac{1}{2}$$

The second step is to add the length of the tenons and an allowance for waste to the visible length. This gives the length of the turning blank that you will need for the center stretcher. Each tenon is 1¼ in. long and I allow ½ in. for waste, so for the example given above, I would cut the turning blank 17½ in. long:

$$14\frac{1}{2} + 2\frac{1}{2} + \frac{1}{2} = 17\frac{1}{2}$$

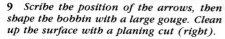
9 *Scribe the position of the arrows, then shape the bobbin with a large gouge. Clean up the surface with a planing cut (right).*

Turning Begin the center stretcher by turning a cylinder of the diameter of the stretcher at its thickest point, which is the center of the bobbin. Make a scribe mark at the center with dividers as described for side stretchers (**8**). Remember to allow for the tenon. The center bobbin slopes down to meet tapered, arrow-shaped turnings at each end. Set calipers to the largest diameter of the arrows and reduce the blank on either side of the center scribe to that diameter using a large gouge. This will begin to create the bobbin.

Next, set a second pair of dividers to the distance from the center scribe to the beginning of the arrows. (Keep the first pair of dividers set to one-half the stretcher's visible length—you will need this pair to mark the tenons.) Scribe these points on the blank with the dividers (**9**).

Shape the bobbin with a large gouge, using the same method as for the side stretchers. Here, however, you work only to the scribes for the arrows. Set calipers to check the diameter of the bobbin where it meets the arrows. Square up the right-angled stops that separate each arrow and the bobbin with a skew. Use the same cut as for cleaning up the last inch or so of the foot of the baluster leg. Clean up the bobbin by making a planing cut with the large skew.

10 *Cut a cove at the beginning of each arrow with a small gouge.*

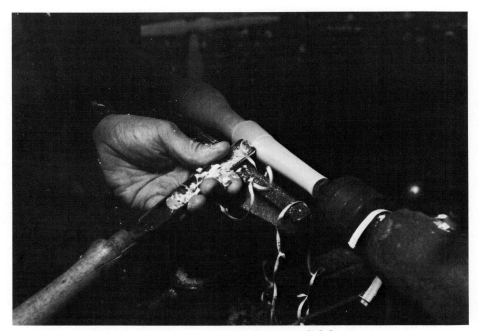

11 *Turn the arrows with a large gouge; make the tapers slightly concave.*

Soften each stop by making a small cove cut with a ¼-in. gouge (**10**). Then, shape each tapered arrow from the cove to the end of the turning blank (**11**). The taper is very slightly concave, another example of reverse entasis (p. 39). The arrows should reduce to ¾ in. in diameter at each end. Scribe the tenon shoulders with the dividers, and cut the tenons in the same manner as for the side stretchers (**12**).

The seven parts that will be used below the seat are now complete. If you turned the armposts and short spindles while making the legs, you will not need to return to the lathe. Drying is all that remains before assembling the seat, legs and stretchers.

Drying the Tenons

The center stretcher has no sockets, so it can be dried in an oven. (I also dry the armposts and short spindles at the same time. They will be assembled later, with the chair back.) I set the temperature for about 175° and leave the parts in for an afternoon. It will take a long time to dry the parts if the temperature setting is too low. On the other hand, I do not want to burn the wood or cause it to honeycomb internally as a result of being dried too quickly. (In practice, the parts stay in the oven until I remember that they are there. This means that my wife regularly stumbles across them at dinner time.)

12 *Scribe the tenon shoulders and turn locking rings on the slightly oversized tenons.*

The tenons of the side stretchers and legs must also be dry, but the body of each part contains a socket that must remain wet. To allow for this, I dry only the tenons by immersing them in hot sand. Just prior to assembling the undercarriage, I heat a cooking pot full of sand. I know it is at the desired temperature when I can spit into the sand and the spit quickly evaporates. I usually make two chairs at once, and the eight legs and four stretchers may take as long as an hour to dry. It's not a quick in-and-out operation.

The tenons should be totally immersed in the sand. Regularly rotate the legs and agitate them in the sand to prevent them from burning. If you withdraw one of the parts, you can watch the water vapor rise out of the end grain of the hot tenon. The tenon should be too hot to touch, but not hot enough to burn the wood. The end of the tenon first loses moisture around its circumference. The dry area continues to expand until only the center of the end grain is still moist. Eventually, this moisture disappears, too.

The later stages of drying are accompanied by pleasant smells. I associate the smells of maple and birch with honeyed toast and that of oak with baked apples. A light tan color on the tenon's surface indicates it is time to stop. If the part is left in the sand any longer, it will burn. You do not need to tend the legs and stretchers constantly while they are in the sand, but check them regularly.

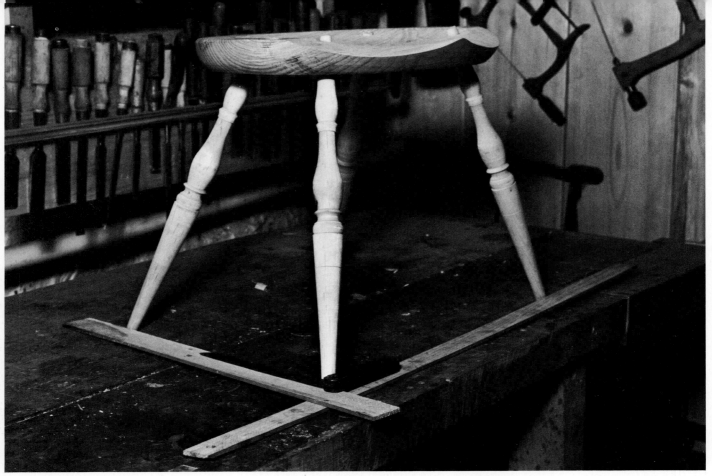

13 *Determine the angle at which the center stretcher meets the side stretchers with two straightedges.*

Assembly

When the center stretcher and the tenons of the legs and side stretchers are dry, the undercarriage is ready for assembly. It is my habit to bore the sockets for the stretcher tenons as I assemble. There is no reason why you cannot bore the sockets all at once. I judge the angles of the sockets by eye. In the beginning, you may feel more comfortable using some measuring devices. I will describe these as I go along.

Insert the four legs into the seat. Set the partially assembled chair upright on a benchtop and find two straightedges. Yardsticks are good. Set one stick flat on the bench with one edge against the two front feet. Place the second against the front and rear feet on one side (**13**). The sticks intersect at the same angle at which the center stretcher is joined to the side stretchers. Set a bevel square to this angle.

Put one side stretcher in a vise so that its length is vertical. The socket is bored on the scribe mark that indicates the center of the bobbin. The location of the socket in relation to the grain is important. As I mentioned in Chapter II, the socket should be bored at a right angle to the wood's layers of annual growth, where the shrinkage will be greatest. For oak, you can locate the rays on the end grain and bore the socket parallel to them.

I prefer to use an easier method of determining where to bore the socket. A turning is shaped in the lathe by cutting through the growth layers. The effect is very much like exposing strata in a hillside. On the bobbin of the stretcher, the desired spot for the socket is indicated by a series of concentric ovals, as shown in the drawing on the facing page. On a tapered foot, these exposed layers of growth form arrows pointing to where the socket should be bored. As you become more experienced at positioning the sockets, your eye will automatically look for these patterns and you will save much of the time usually spent rethinking the dynamics of shrinking wood.

When the location of the socket is selected, bore the hole, using the bevel square to check the angle. Hold the head of the brace against your stomach to steady it. Start the spoon bit at a right angle to the stretcher. Then set the blade of the bevel square against the stretcher, parallel to an imaginary centerline. Raise the brace until its centerline corresponds to the stock of the bevel square and bore the socket (**14**). I have filed a mark on the back of the spoon bit used to make the leg sockets. The mark, 1¼ in. from the nose of the bit, tells me when I have bored as deeply as I can without coming through the other side.

14 *You can use a bevel square to help determine the angle of the brace and bit while boring the center-stretcher socket in a side stretcher.*

15 *Make a gauge from a piece of scrap wood to check the size of each stretcher tenon before assembly. If the tenon is too thick, trim its lobes with a chisel.*

The socket is angled only to the length of the stretcher and bisects the thickness. You might want to check with the bevel square before completing the socket to make sure that the bit has not wandered; you can easily remember the location of the head of the brace against your belly. This reference point makes it easy to re-establish the correct angle. The tolerances for the undercarriage sockets are wide, because the stretchers are still green and flexible. In fact, some slight error can be beneficial, because the error will create tension in the undercarriage. However, there can be too much of a good thing.

Before assembling the side stretcher and center stretcher, check the size of the center-stretcher tenon. The oversized tenons shrink when dried in the hot sand, but they might not shrink enough to fit the sockets. It is best to find out if a tenon is too thick before you try to assemble a joint. Bore a hole into a block of seasoned hardwood with the ⅝-in. spoon bit. A tenon should fit snugly into this hole (15). If it is too tight, shave the lobes with a chisel until it fits. Quickly check the tenon with this gauge before assembling each joint.

Positioning Sockets

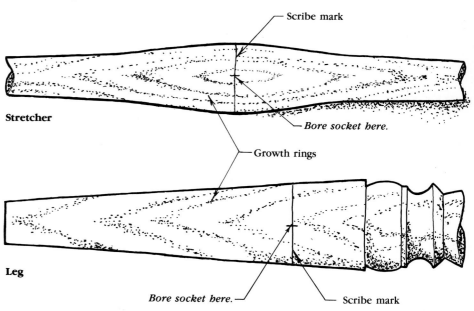

Scribe mark

Stretcher

Bore socket here.

Growth rings

Leg

Bore socket here.

Scribe mark

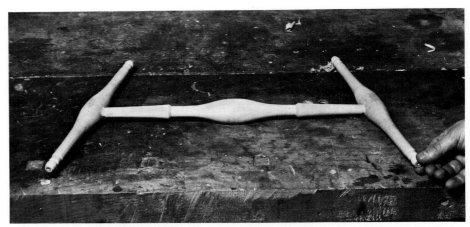

17 *The assembled stretchers should all lie in the same plane.*

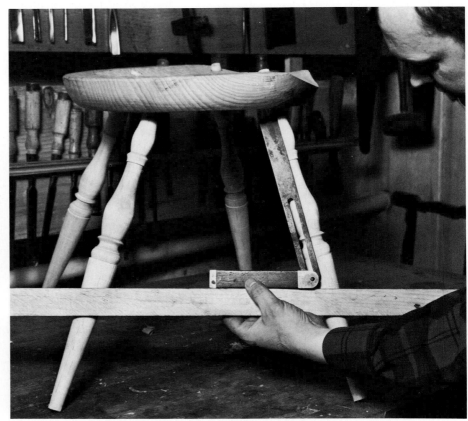

18 *Place a straightedge between a front and back leg at the height of the scribe marks to determine the angle of the side stretcher to each of the legs.*

16 *Rotate the first side stretcher as you push it onto the center stretcher.*

Remove the side stretcher from the vise and assemble it and the center stretcher. Squirt some glue into the socket. Smear the glue uniformly over the sides of the socket with a small stick. Insert one of the center-stretcher tenons into the socket. It should fit tightly. Rotate the side stretcher as you press it onto the tenon (**16**).

Bore the socket in the second side stretcher and mount it on the other end of the center stretcher in the same way. Twist the side stretchers so that the three pieces form a plane. Place them on the benchtop to test this (**17**).

Next, you need to find the angle at which the legs are mounted on the side stretchers. Place a straightedge against one front leg and its corresponding rear leg at the height of the scribe marks. Set bevel squares to the angles formed by the staightedge and the legs (**18**). Using two bevel squares will save you from having to reset a single bevel after boring the front-leg sockets.

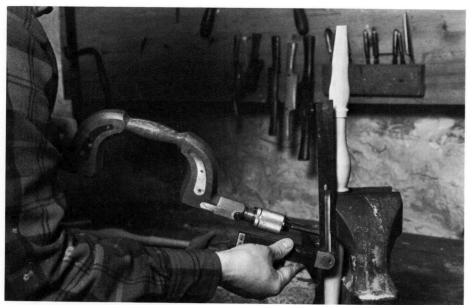

19 *Establish the correct angle for boring the stretcher socket by holding a bevel square against the leg and the brace and bit.*

20 *Insert the leg into the seat and pull the stretcher assembly into position. The center stretcher should be parallel to the seat.*

Armed with this information, put one of the front legs in the vise. Start the socket at a right angle to the leg. Place the blade or the stock of the bevel square parallel to an imaginary centerline of the leg and bring the brace up to the proper angle (**19**). Bore the socket. You may want to check for wandering before completing the hole. Put glue in the socket and mount the leg onto the appropriate side-stretcher tenon with the same twisting and pressing motion as was used in joining the stretchers.

The angle of the leg in relation to the plane of the stretchers is critical. Put the leg tenon into its socket in the seat (don't glue it), and pull the stretcher assembly down until the center stretcher is parallel to the plane of the seat (**20**). The tenon of the side stretcher should twist in the leg socket to allow this movement. The side stretchers may or may not be parallel to the seat, depending on the rake of the leg.

Turning the Stretchers and Assembling the Undercarriage **65**

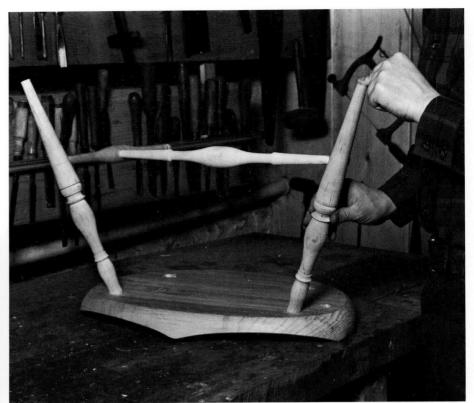

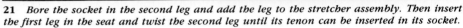

21 *Bore the socket in the second leg and add the leg to the stretcher assembly. Then insert the first leg in the seat and twist the second leg until its tenon can be inserted in its socket.*

22 *Twist the first rear leg onto its stretcher tenon. Then rotate the leg into its socket.*

Remove the assembly from the seat and bore, glue and mount the second leg on the appropriate side-stretcher tenon. Put the tenon of the first leg back in its socket, and twist the second leg until its tenon can be inserted into its socket in the seat (**21**).

Next, bore the socket in the first rear leg. If you are using only one bevel square, remember to reset its angle for the rear legs. Put glue in the socket in the leg and mount it on the side-stretcher tenon. Insert the two front legs in their sockets and rotate the rear leg until its tenon fits into the corresponding seat socket (**22**).

Perform the same operations on the last leg. However, when it is twisted into position, this leg will not readily fall into its socket. Instead, it will meet the seat at a point slightly behind that socket. This is because the stretchers were made ¼ in. overlong, which spreads the legs apart. If the assembled legs and stretchers are lowered onto the seat together, each tenon will be just slightly off the mark (**23**). Forcing the tenons home will create the tension in the undercarriage that helps make the chair durable.

23 *The legs will not line up with their sockets because of the extra length of the stretchers. When the tenons are forced into their sockets during final assembly, each leg will be stressed equally.*

24 *After inserting the legs, rap their ends sharply with a hammer to set the tenons firmly in the seat sockets.*

Remove the undercarriage from the seat. You want to work quickly and assuredly at this point. Remember that glue will be setting up in the joints. There is, however, no reason to hurry and risk a mistake. Squirt glue into the sockets for the legs in the seat and spread it evenly on the socket walls before it has a chance to run out. Place the seat top down on the bench. Hold the front pair of legs near the tenons. Draw the tenons together; this will stress the stretcher-to-leg joints slightly. When the tenons are at the same angles as the sockets, insert them with a snap of the wrists. This locks them in place. Do the same to the back pair of legs. These tenons must be squeezed together and pulled toward the front legs to fit their sockets. Because of the extra length of the stretchers, the entire undercarriage is now under a slight tension.

Lift up the seat to check that the top ends of all four tenons are exposed above the surface of the seat. The legs are now ready to be set a final time. Sharply rap the foot end of each leg with a hammer (**24**). You want the joint to be tight, but do not risk splitting the seat. Be cautious—if driven with too much force, a tapered tenon can also act as a wedge.

26 *Make a split for the wedge in the end of the tenon with a chisel. The split should follow the direction of the grain in the leg. It should be at about a right angle to the grain of the seat.*

25 *Shape a wedge on the end of a dry, riven hardwood stick. The wedge should be slightly wider than the socket, and it should taper slightly in its width, as well as its thickness (right).*

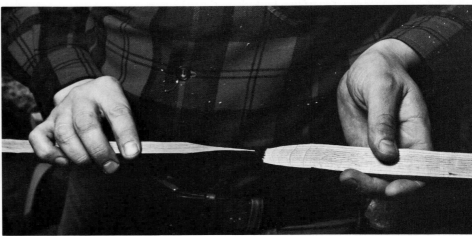

When the tenons have been set, place the chair upright. You need to wedge the tenons before the glue begins to set. A wedge performs several tasks. It spreads the tenon so that a good, tight glue bond is achieved. It produces a flare at the top of the tenon so that when the joint does loosen, the tenon will not fall out of the socket. The wedge should also completely close the joint on the top surface of the seat, so that no visible gap remains between tenon and socket.

Some people make a separate, individual wedge for each joint. I have never understood why. I cut a wedge on one end of a stick, drive the wedge in, cut the stick off and then make another wedge on the same end. There is little wasted wood or effort. The stick is steadily whittled down to a stub, like a pencil, and it is run through the stove when it becomes too short to hold. I keep a supply of riven oak sticks for wedges stored over a heat duct. These are leftovers from riving spindles. If a riven piece is too thin or otherwise unacceptable for spindles, I set it above the duct where it can dry. By doing this, I always have dry wood on hand to use for wedges.

I cut wedges with a drawknife. One end of the stick is held in my tin-knocker's vise while I work the wedge on the other (**25**). The wedges should be slightly wider than the sockets. The edges of the wedge will bite into the soft pine, producing the keying effect mentioned in Chapter II. A keyed wedge will prevent the tenon from slipping due to torque. Taper the width of the wedge as well as its thickness. This taper makes the end of the wedge narrower than the tenon, so it is easier to start in the split. As the wedge enters the split, it becomes wider and will gradually bite into the softer pine.

27   *Drive the wedge with sharp raps of a hammer.*

Make a split for the wedge in the end of the tenon. I make the split with a chisel driven by my cobbler's hammer. You must be ever conscious when wedging that it is possible to split the seat. For this reason, you should wedge at a right angle to the grain (**26**). However, this placement does not always close gaps on the surface of the seat between the tenon and the socket. You can revolve the chisel on the end grain of the leg tenon to position the split so that the wedge will close these gaps. Once again, there is a possibility of too much of a good thing. A slight gap is better than a seat that has been broken into two pieces. (If the joint will not close by repositioning the split, it can be double-wedged. Drive in the first wedge at about 45° to the grain, then add a second wedge at a right angle to the first to close the gap.)

Drive the wedge by rapping the end of the stick with a hammer (**27**). The joint will supply its own signal when the wedge is driven home. As the wedge is driven, it vibrates and gives off a short hum like a plucked guitar string. Each blow of the hammer shortens the stick and lowers the pitch of the sound. The pitch decreases until several blows produce only a dead knock. This sound indicates that the wedge is not moving anymore. Stop driving now, because any further movement may split the seat.

Cut the stick loose with a saw, and form a new wedge on its end. Wedge the remaining joints in the same way.

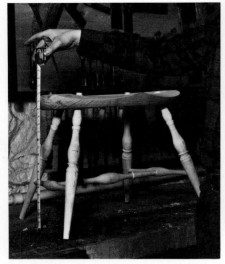

28 *To trim the front legs, measure the height of the seat at the pommel and at each armpost (top left). Calculate how much to cut off and mark the legs (top right). Trim with a backsaw, holding it parallel to the benchtop (bottom).*

29 *Hang the last leg over the benchtop to determine its correct length. You can use the benchtop as a guide for sawing.*

Trimming the Legs

The undercarriage and seat are assembled, but the legs do not yet sit squarely on the bench. They must be cut to length. This recalls the old vaudeville routine in which a poor fellow tries to cut all the legs of a chair to the same length and ends up with a seat sitting on stubs only a couple of inches high. If he had used the following method, he would have got it right the first time.

I cut the legs of both chairs so that the seats are about ½ in. lower at the back than the front. This slope adds to the chair's comfort, and I like the way a sloped seat looks.

Start by measuring the height of the seat pommel above the bench. For example, let's say that this measurement is 18¼ in. Next, measure the height of the seat near each armpost (**28**). Let's say that the right side is 17¾ in. and the left is 18¼ in. I like the pommel of all my chairs to be about 17 in. above the floor, so the leg on the highest side must be lowered 1¼ in. Measure from the benchtop up 1¼ in. on the taper of the left leg and make a mark.

If you also cut 1¼ in. off the leg on the lower side, however, the front edge of the seat will not be level. Cutting ¾ in. off the right leg, and 1¼ in. off the left should bring the pommel down to about 17 in., and make the front of the seat level. Measure up from the bench for the right leg and cut the excess length off each leg with a backsaw. Be careful to keep the blade of the saw parallel with the surface of the bench.

At this point, only one of the back legs usually touches the bench. This can occur for a variety of reasons. One rear socket may have been reamed more deeply than the other. One tenon may have been formed slightly further up the minor vase. Or, one rake angle may be slightly greater than the other. It doesn't matter anyway, as the rear legs also get trimmed.

If the pommel is 17 in. high, the height of the seat at the back should be about 16½ in. high. Let's say that the right leg as you face the back is longer than the left, and the back surface of the seat is currently 17½ in. above the bench. Mark 1 in. up on the taper of the right leg and cut off the excess. The chair now rests on the left leg, which is still too long.

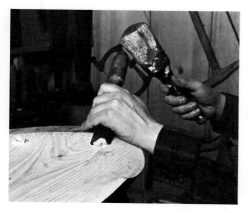

30 *A wide, shallow carving gouge works well to trim the tenon ends flush with the surface of the seat.*

31 *The assembled seat and undercarriage.*

To cut off the correct amount on the last leg, hang it over the edge of the bench (**29**). The seat now rests on the three legs that have been measured and cut to correct length. The edge of the benchtop intersects the fourth leg at precisely the correct location for the final cut. Mark this point and cut it with the backsaw, or cut using the benchtop as a guide.

Only one more detail remains. The ends of the leg tenons need to be shaved flush with the surface of the seat. I don't do this earlier because the seat will not sit squarely before the legs are trimmed to length; uneven legs make the seat difficult to hold still. I use a wide, shallow carving gouge to trim the tenons flush. I drive it with a mallet, cutting across the end grain (**30**). You know what happens when you plane end grain—the last little bit tears or breaks off. The same danger exists when flushing the tenons. Therefore, chop through only about two thirds of the tenon from one direction. Then work back toward the middle from the other side. After most of the waste has been removed, put down the mallet and trim the tenon flush with a slicing cut, holding the blade at an extreme skew to the direction of the cut. Trim all four tenons the same way.

Eventually, the ends of the tenons will probably rise above the surface of the seat. This occurs for a number of reasons. During the first year, the hardwood tenons may be driven by use further into the softwood sockets, pushing the ends slightly above the seat. Throughout the life of the chair, expansion and contraction of the seat and legs with seasonal humidity changes may sometimes cause the ends to pop up more. It's futile to try to trim the tenons so that they will always be flush. If you trim them flush when the seat has shrunk, they will just be recessed when the seat has swollen again. Therefore, I think it is best to trim the ends at assembly, then leave them alone. The exposed top of the leg tenon is part of the nature of the beast.

Chapter VI

Bending the Backs

With the base of the chair finished, you are ready to make the back. It is the back that distinguishes one Windsor from another, as is reflected in the nomenclature—low back, high back, sack back, oval back, continuous arm, and so on. Most types of Windsors have at least one piece of bent wood in their backs. The sack-back chair has a bent arm and bent bow. The bow is joined to the arm, and both parts are connected by spindles to the seat. Both are *U*-shaped and are bent on the same form. The continuous-arm chair has a single back piece bent in two planes. Because of its compound shape, this piece is more difficult to bend than those for the sack back. In this chapter, I will describe how to bend all three of these pieces.

Wood Selection

Perhaps no single aspect of Windsor chairmaking is as challenging as is bending the pieces for the back. The most important factor in bending is wood selection. Bending is alien to the nature of wood. Being heated and then suddenly contorted are assaults that wood does not accept without some reluctance. The bending process creates tremendous strains that only the best pieces of wood can be expected to survive. Therefore, do not waste your time working wood that does not meet the standards I am going to describe.

I regularly receive telephone calls from people who are having trouble bending the back for a Windsor chair. The caller will explain that he has selected the best piece of wood he can find, and his bows still break. When I ask where the wood is coming from, the answer is invariably a local lumber dealer. I have learned not to speak in absolutes, but on this matter I come very close: Do not try to bend sawn wood from a lumberyard. It is a waste of time. The best blanks for bending are riven directly from the log. A saw pays no attention to the direction of the wood fibers—the grain of a sawn piece will not run uninterrupted from end to end. Furthermore, wood purchased from a lumberyard has usually been kiln-dried. I have noticed that kiln-dried wood feels more brittle when working it than air-dried wood. I know of no one who is regularly able to bend the stuff successfully.

Although many species of wood can be rived, steamed and bent successfully, my preferred wood is red oak. I can perhaps most easily explain why I prefer this wood by first describing the problems I have had with others.

Hickory While still green, hickory is a delight to work. Billets that do not contain any knots and that have straight grain split with ease. The fresh wood is as soft as butter; it cuts cleanly and shaves easily.

When steamed, hickory does not soften or plasticize as much as do some other species. However, the wood is so tough when green that it can actually be bent without first being steamed. In other words, unseasoned hickory will bend cold. This process requires mechanical assistance. After a piece of cold-bent hickory has cured, it will retain its shape, but I caution against being in the way if a cold-bent hickory bow should slip lose from its bending form before curing. It will give you a good knock.

Once hickory has seasoned, it is difficult to work. It takes on an almost metallic hardness, and a great deal of effort is required just to bore a hole through it. The bent parts of Windsor backs require a lot of holes to house the spindles, so this characteristic is undesirable. Seasoned hickory is also less flexible than red oak and it tends to be more brittle.

Fresh-cut hickory billets dry quickly, and their ends develop large checks, even if painted. Therefore, hickory has a short shelf life. If kept on hand more than a couple of weeks, it either spoils due to checking or dries to a point where it is unworkable.

White ash When green, white ash also splits cleanly and easily, and it whittles and planes easily. Steamed, it plasticizes and bends without too much effort. However, it dries to a metallic hardness, too, and is difficult to work.

Ash does not check as badly as hickory when drying. When left in the log, ash is attacked by a fungus that breaks down the wood so that it shears easily across the grain when stressed. The fungus is indicated by a spotted, light blue stain in the sapwood. To prevent this fungus attack, it is necessary to quarter the log and remove the bark. Of course, the smaller pieces of wood will season more rapidly.

I have observed a curious phenomenon in ash. I once set aside some ash quarters that became quite workable a year or so later. They split well, worked with reasonable ease and bent nicely.

White oak Second-growth white oak trees tend to branch fairly low. The result is a short trunk in which the layers of annual growth are deflected near the stump and lower limbs. Such trees do not contain as much serviceable bending stock, which must be straight-grained, as do taller trees.

Of the woods discussed thus far, white oak is often the most difficult to split. Unlike hickory and ash, it does not usually pop open cleanly under the force of a wedge. Instead, wood fibers pull loose from both sides of the split. Dozens of these fibers, each the thickness of a pencil, hold the halves together and must be snipped with a hatchet to separate the pieces. These torn fibers ruin the surrounding wood that could otherwise be made into backs.

White oak also becomes difficult to work as it hardens. It is a great firewood, but I pass on white oak when it comes to making chair backs.

1 *To split a 5-ft.-long, red oak log for chair backs, begin the split by driving a wedge into the edge of one end. Add a second wedge near the heart.*

Red oak   The troubles I have described above can be avoided by using red oak for bending. This species often grows 20 ft. to 30 ft. before branching. A good forest tree is as straight as an arrow, and its trunk will render several logs suitable for chair backs. There is enough stock in one good red oak tree to keep me busy for as long as two years. (In practice, I do not use wood that old. I reorder fresh logs twice a year. Last season's oak is next winter's firewood.)

A good red oak log will split open as easily as hickory or ash. After several blows of the maul, the log signals its surrender with a resounding pop. When the two halves fall apart, I have to skip quickly to protect my ankles. Another nice feature of red oak is its bark. It has a texture that is a portrait of the log's interior. Any deflection or distortion in the grain around an enclosed blemish will show up on the bark.

After several months in warm weather, the sapwood of a red oak log will also be invaded by a staining fungus. Red oak attacked by fungus will show a speckling of light blue stains in the sapwood, and will also shear at a right angle to the grain when being bent. To avoid fungus attack, I split the log into sections about 4 in. square and remove the bark. These sections are either taken into the shop or stored outside, off the ground. They will make up a season's supply of backs. When firewood is being stacked for next year, they will be replaced with freshly split sections.

As soon as the oak is brought into the shop, it begins to dry. As the year progresses, the wood contains less and less moisture. This is not a problem with red oak—when bending, you just steam it longer to bring up the moisture content. It does harden somewhat as it seasons, but it never takes on the almost

metallic hardness of hickory, ash or white oak. When a bent part is hung up to dry, it will not become too hard to plane, scrape, saw or bore easily.

There is only one problem with red oak. It contains tannic acid, which causes the wood to stain a purple color when it comes in contact with a ferrous metal. This stain is never very deep and it is easily removed with a cabinet scraper. Red oak also takes on a slight greyish cast after it has been steamed. This color is permanent, but most people will not notice it if it's not pointed out. I always recommend paint as the appropriate finish for a Windsor, and if this advice is followed, this slight discoloration is nothing to worry about.

Red oak grows nearly everywhere east of the Mississippi. If it is not native to your region, you will have to experiment until you find a species with the same qualities.

2 Halve, then quarter the log (above and right). Notice the deflected grain near the heartwood. The successive annual growth toward the outside of the log becomes straighter. This is why logs at least 12 in. in diameter are best for chairmaking.

3 For a log this size, eighths are about the smallest parts that need to be split with the maul and wedges.

4 After riving, strip the bark off the red oak billets with a drawknife.

Riving and Shaping

Whether you use red oak or a comparable species, it is important to select a good log. The grain of the blanks you rive from it must be sound and run uninterrupted from one end to the other. A blank should be straight with no distortion. A slight curve is acceptable, but the grain cannot be deflected anywhere along its length. Curly grain, pin knots, ingrown bark or any other blemishes are unacceptable.

When you have selected the log, saw it to length. Sack-back bows and arms can be got out of 4-ft.-long sections, continuous arms from sections 5 ft. long.

Split the log into billets that are small enough to be easily handled and transported. I often split a log into eighths (1,2,3). At this point, I cease working outside and go into the shop. One of the eighths should yield enough material for at least one, but probably two or more chair backs. Remove the bark from the billet with a drawknife (4). The bark must be taken off before any further work is done. If left on the wood, it will sometimes cause a split to run where you do not want it to go. Also, the bark can hide the split and you will not be able to watch it. (If you are storing the remaining billets for future chairs, remember to drawknife the bark off them to prevent fungus from forming.) Next, remove the pith, as well as a couple of inches of surrounding wood by riving it from the billet. There are usually pin knots and deflected grain in this area.

5 *After removing the bark and pith from a billet, sketch out the back blanks on an end for riving.*

6 *Hold the billet vertically and rive the back blanks with a hatchet driven by a maul. Always split so there are pieces of equal mass on each side of the hatchet.*

With a pencil, sketch on the end grain the number of back blanks that you can obtain from this billet (**5**). I rive blanks for the sack-back bow and for the continuous arm about 1⅛ in. square. A blank for a sack-back arm is about 1⅛ in. by ¾ in. I want each piece of riven stock to be close to the final dimensions of the back piece. Riving is not as accurate as sawing, and can be difficult to control when working to close tolerances. The nearer you try to size each blank to its finished dimensions, the more you risk making it too small. I am happy if 75% of the blanks that I sketch out are usable.

The rule for splitting bending blanks is the same as for splitting turning stock: Always split pieces of equal mass. If you try to rive a thin piece from a large billet, the split will run out in the direction of the smaller mass.

I use a Kent hatchet, wooden maul and a froe to rive the backs. Place the oak vertically. I hold it upright in my bench vise. Start the split with the hatchet and maul (**6**). The hatchet head may become buried so that it cannot be driven with the maul; when this happens, I insert a froe below the hatchet to complete the split (**7**). This simple tool has a long metal blade that is wedge-shaped in cross section. Its wooden handle is set into an eye on one end of the blade and at a right angle to the blade's length. The handle functions as a lever, and allows you to work the blade back and forth when opening a split.

7 *A froe is handy for splitting long pieces. Using the handle as a lever, work the blade back and forth to control the split as it opens. The wedge-shaped blade can also be driven into the end grain to start a split.*

8 *You can try to redirect a split that is running out by driving the edge of the hatchet into the billet in the direction the split should go.*

The first split in a 4-in. by 4-in. billet is usually easy. Any trouble will occur riving the final pieces. I find it easier to control the split in a narrow piece if I take the piece in hand and drop its lower end on the floor. The resulting shock opens the split more gently and with more control than can be obtained by striking the hatchet with the maul. If the split begins to run out, turn the piece around and split from the other end. If this does not work, you can try to re-establish the split from the middle of the billet (**8**). Rest the billet on a chopping block. Set the cutting edge of the hatchet on it in the direction that the split should be going. Give the

hatchet a sharp rap with a maul to drive the edge into the grain. If you are lucky, the hatchet's edge will pick up the split and redirect it.

It may sound like you will have to struggle with the wood. I have described the worst case, run-out, and its remedy. Most pieces open just as nicely as could please and split to size with no trouble at all.

A question that I am invariably asked is "Why can't I cut the blanks on a tablesaw?" The problem with sawing is that the saw ignores the direction of grain. If there is a long, gentle bow in the oak billet, riving will follow that arc and still render a serviceable back blank. A tablesaw is oblivious to grain direction, and cuts a straight line that severs the grain along the way. You will not even save time by sawing. I can split out back blanks as fast as they could be sawn, and I am assured of their quality.

9 *To shape the sack-back arm, remove the bulk of the waste from the blank with a drawknife. Then, plane the blank to its finished dimension.*

Shaping the sack back Once you have split the blanks out near to size, trim the bow blank 45 in. long and the arm blank 44 in. long. Then begin to shape them. The first tool I use is a drawknife. The drawknife is a roughing tool, and I only rely on it to hew off the bulk of the waste. I can easily take off shavings that are the full width of the piece and as thick as a pencil.

Drawknife the arm blank roughly rectangular in section (**9**). Once you have removed most of the waste, clamp the blank on a workbench and finish up the four sides with a smoothing plane to the final ½-in. by ¾-in. cross section. The unseasoned oak blank will plane cleanly and easily.

The bow can also be rounded roughly with the drawknife. I maintain a constant ¾-in. diameter by passing the bow through a gauge. The gauge is no more than a small block of wood with a ¾-in. hole bored through it. Move the gauge along the developing bow to find the high spots (**10**). It will not pass over these places, and they must be trimmed down. I do this with a forkstaff plane (**11**). This plane looks like a smoothing plane, but has a concave sole that makes it very useful for rounding parts such as bows. You can also round the bow with a spokeshave.

10 *Round the bow blank with a drawknife. Make a simple gauge to check the diameter of the bow as you go along.*

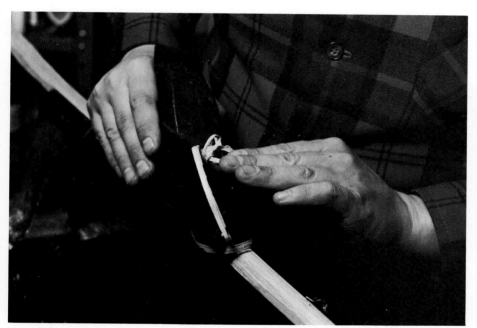

11 *A forkstaff plane, which is a smoothing plane with a concave sole, is useful for finishing the round bow.*

12 *Taper the ends of the bow from ¾ in. to ⅜ in. in diameter with a drawknife.*

When the entire length of the bow will travel through the gauge, place the bow in a vise and taper both ends with the drawknife (**12**). The last 6 in. of the bow decrease in diameter from ¾ in. to ⅜ in. This is the size of the socket for joining the bow to the arm. Leave the ends slightly oversized and do not do any finish-smoothing or scraping at this time. The bow still must be bent, and there is always a risk that it will break. If it breaks, you will throw away all the extra finishing work.

Finally, locate and mark the center of the lengths of the arm and bow. You will need these marks later to position the pieces on the bending form.

13 *After riving, select the face of the continuous-arm blank and plane it flat.*

14 *With the blank held face down in a vise, drawknife the ends ⁷⁄₁₆ in. thick.*

Shaping the continuous arm The continuous arm is a more complex shape. The arm is curved in two planes. The center of the arm is in one plane that is more or less vertical and is supported above the seat by the long spindles. The arm curves at each end into a horizontal plane. These end segments, which support the sitter's arms, are fixed to the seat by the armposts and short spindles. In each plane, the arm has a distinct cross section. The center segment, in the vertical plane, is a square of about ¾ in. on a side. Its back surface is slightly rounded, as shown in the drawing on p. 145. The end segments, those in the horizontal plane, are about ⁷⁄₁₆ in. thick. They also become wider, enlarging from ¾ in. to about 1⅛ in. wide at each end.

Trim the blank 56 in. long. Then examine it to decide which surface will be the face. The face is the surface that you see when looking at the chair from the front. It is the surface that supports the sitter's back and elbows. I look for two things when selecting the face. If one surface of the blank widens at its ends, I choose that surface for the face, because these flaring ends will make shaping the hands easier. If no surface is flared, I select the one that split most cleanly. A cleanly split surface can be planed easily and quickly. When you have selected the face, clamp the blank to the benchtop and plane the face flat, so its entire surface lies more or less in a single plane (**13**). (The drawing on the facing page shows the steps in shaping the continuous arm.)

Next, lay out marks on the back surface of the blank to help when developing the changing cross sections of the arm. Locate and mark the center of the blank, 28 in. from either end. Mark a line 14 in. on each side of the center. This divides the blank into the center and two end segments.

Place the blank, face down, in a vise and then pare the two end segments to ⁷⁄₁₆ in. thick with the drawknife (**14**). The transition from middle to end segments is a short taper. When this waste is removed, the blank will approximate its finished shape. There is now no doubt which of the surfaces is the face and which is the back.

Clamp the blank on the bench and plane one edge square to the face. (If the blank has flared ends, plane the edge opposite the flared edge now.) This will be the inside edge of the vertical center segment. It will be placed against the curved form when bending. Next, plane the back surface to make the center segment ¾ in. thick.

The remaining edge will be flat along the length of the center segment and flare out so the blank is wider at both ends. Plane this final edge to make the center segment of the blank ¾ in. square, and taper the end segments into the center. To do this, you will need a plane that has a short sole, such as a smoothing plane. A plane with a longer sole will not allow you to shape the flared ends.

The square center segment does not have four sharp arrises. The two on the back surface are gently rounded. I do this with the forkstaff plane (**15**). You could use a smoothing plane or a spokeshave. Next, clean up the transition on the back surface from the center segment to the thinner ends. Make the transition taper gradually over a couple of inches. This is a short area and it is end grain, so I use a spokeshave (**16**). Locate and mark with a pencil the exact center of the arm. (Your original marks were probably removed during shaping.) Mark also the inside edge of the arm. These marks will position the piece on the bending form.

15 *Round the arrises of the center segment with a forkstaff plane (shown here), a spokeshave or smoothing plane.*

16 *Soften the transition from the center segment to each end with a spokeshave.*

Shaping the Continuous Arm

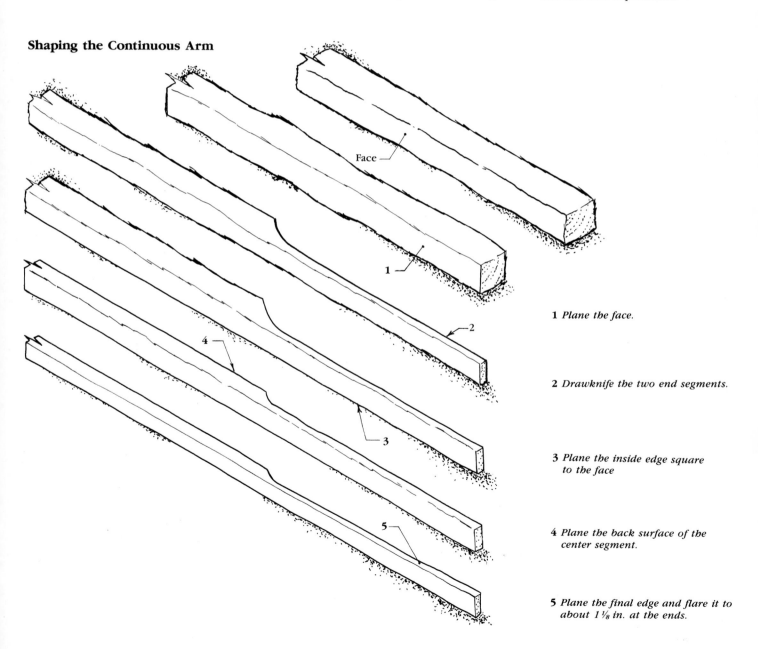

Face

1

2

4

3

5

1 *Plane the face.*

2 *Drawknife the two end segments.*

3 *Plane the inside edge square to the face*

4 *Plane the back surface of the center segment.*

5 *Plane the final edge and flare it to about 1 ⅛ in. at the ends.*

Bending the Backs   **81**

17 *A simple steambox consists of a PVC pipe, two aluminum kettles and a camp stove. The steam from the kettles rises into the pipe through two plastic hoses.*

Steaming and Bending

Almost every procedure in the making of a chair relies on skill to ensure success. For example, when I start a seat, I am almost certain that when I am done I will have an acceptable part. The only possibility for failure is an unnoticed flaw in the wood itself. Bending, however, is not as certain. In spite of the knowledge gained from having made countless bends, I still occasionally lose a bow or an arm. The sickening sound of rending wood is in my mind's ear as I state that bending requires as much intuition as skill.

Two elements are necessary for successful steam-bending: moisture and heat. If both are present in sufficient quantities, the wood will soften to a hard-rubberlike state. In this state, the wood is said to be plasticized. If either moisture or heat is absent, the wood will not bend, regardless of how much of the other is applied. The wood could be soaked until waterlogged, but it would break if not sufficiently hot. It could be heated to nearly the flash point, but without the required amount of moisture, it would not tolerate the stresses of bending.

To bend, the parts for the chair backs must have about 20% to 25% moisture content and be heated to about 180°F. Unseasoned oak or other suitable and unseasoned species should already contain sufficient water; the problem is to raise the temperature. This could be done by boiling the wood in some sort of container, but you would have to find a suitable tub. This method would also require boiling a relatively large amount of water. I prefer to steam the wood in a small pipe that is only somewhat airtight and that requires you to heat very little water.

The steambox My setup requires two inexpensive aluminum kettles, the type available in any hardware or department store (**17**). The kettles are heated on a gasoline-fired camp stove. A gasoline fire burns blue and boils the liquid much more quickly than would an electric hot plate. The steambox is a 5-ft. length of 4-in.-diameter PVC pipe, used for drain, waste and vent plumbing. A PVC cap is placed over each end of the pipe to contain the steam.

A PVC-pipe steambox is lightweight, easily stored and impervious to rot and mold. PVC is a reasonably good insulator. When my steambox is perking at full tilt, I can easily hold my hand on its surface without discomfort. PVC pipe is also inexpensive and readily available at any plumbing supplier. I use pipe rated Schedule 40, which has walls about ¼ in. thick.

The steam generated in the kettles is carried a short distance up to the pipe through two plastic hoses. I made these from some tubing that came with a sump pump. The same stuff is sold in marinas as bilge-pump hose. One end of each hose is forced over the spout of the kettle. The other end is inserted into a hole bored into the pipe.

The chair parts should be suspended inside the pipe on two ½-in. dowels inserted through the pipe wall. The steam will condense, and water will gather at the bottom of the pipe, so if the parts were laid on the bottom, they would be merely bathed in condensate that is considerably cooler than the steam. The dowels fit into ½-in. holes bored clear through the pipe at two places along its length. These holes are at right angles to the holes for the steam hoses; the ends of the dowels are cut flush with the outside surface of the pipe.

The pipe is suspended above the stove and kettles by resting its ends on two cinder blocks. The pipe should be angled slightly, so the end from which the parts are removed is lower than the other. The condensed steam runs out a ½-in.-diameter hole bored in the bottom of the pipe. Once you have obtained the parts, the whole setup can be assembled in about a half hour. The other piece of equipment that you will need to bend the back of each chair is a bending form.

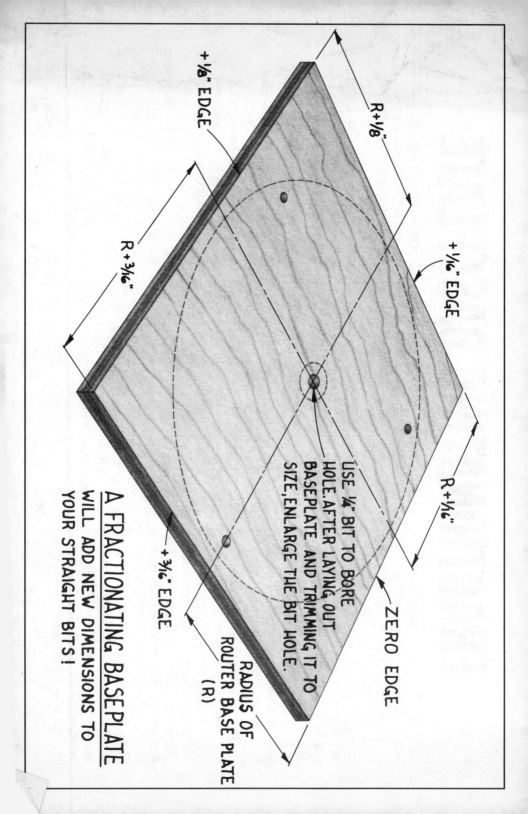

+1/8" EDGE

R+1/8"

+1/16" EDGE

R+3/16"

R+1/16"

USE 1/4" BIT TO BORE
HOLE. AFTER LAYING OUT
BASEPLATE AND TRIMMING IT TO
SIZE, ENLARGE THE BIT HOLE.

+3/16" EDGE

ZERO EDGE

RADIUS OF
ROUTER BASE PLATE
(R)

A FRACTIONATING BASEPLATE
WILL ADD NEW DIMENSIONS TO
YOUR STRAIGHT BITS!

FRACTIONATING BASEPLATE

This baseplate looks like a square, but it's a trickster developed by Nick Engler, one of my favorite woodworking writers. The measurement from the axis of the bit to each of the four baseplate edges is different. With this baseplate, you expand the cutting width of any straight bit in your collection, and you give yourself the ability to produce a greater incremental range of cuts.

Cutting a ⁹⁄₁₆-inch-wide dado, or a ⁵⁄₈-inch-wide dado, or a ¹¹⁄₁₆-inch-wide dado is as simple as turning the router to reference a different edge against the guide fence. Use a ½-inch straight bit and make a pass with the "zero" side against the fence. Then turn the router so the "+ ¹⁄₈" side is against the fence and make a second pass. The additional ¹⁄₈ inch between the bit and the fence adds ¹⁄₈ inch to the width of the cut.

Using a ¾-inch bit with this base gives you dado-widths of ¾ inch, ¹³⁄₁₆ inch, ⅞ inch, and ¹⁵⁄₁₆ inch. A quarter-inch bit yields widths of ¼ inch, ⁵⁄₁₆ inch, ⅜ inch, and ⁷⁄₁₆ inch.

If you are really clever, you'll see that Nick's idea is an inexpensive solution to undersized plywood. One of the shortcomings of plywood, especially hardwood stuff, is that it's often a 64th or a 32nd undersize. Three-quarter ply is more likely ²³⁄₃₂ inch or ⁴⁷⁄₆₄ inch. It rattles in the dado you cut for it with your ¾ inch straight. Maddening.

One solution is to buy special dadoing bits that are ²³⁄₃₂ inch. But a less costly solution is to make a version of this fractionating baseplate that'll allow you to make those off-sized dadoes in two passes with a ½-inch or ⅝-inch bit.

Make a pass with the zero edge against the fence; the cut will match the bit's diameter. Turn the router so a different edge rides the fence and make a second pass. The bit is repositioned farther from the fence, widening the cut.

To make the baseplate, cut a square of plywood or acrylic. Drill mounting holes using the factory baseplate as a template. Screw the acrylic plate to the router and bore a ¼-inch bit hole by switching on the router and advancing the bit into the baseplate. Now, remove the baseplate from the router. Measure from the bit hole to the edges of the baseplate, as indicated in the drawing. Trim the baseplate to produce the desired result. Remount the baseplate and you're ready to cut some odd-size dadoes.

Printed in USA
OSW12986B

18 *A simple sack-back bending form with dowels and wedges for holding the piece in place.*

The sack-back form Both the sack-back arm and bow can be bent on the same simple form made of 2-in.-thick pine or other inexpensive softwood, attached to a backboard of 1-in.-thick plywood (**18**). Cut the pine to the outline of the curve shown on the drawing at right. You can make a pattern by plotting the points and connecting them to form a smooth curve. After cutting the curve, nail the pine securely to the plywood. At the apex of the curve, about 1¼ in. from the pine block, attach a stop made of a small rectangular piece of hardwood with several screws. It should be at least 1 in. thick and securely fastened, because it must endure a lot of strain.

During bending, each end of an arm or bow is held in place by a dowel near the bottom of each side of the pine block. Bore ½-in. holes for these dowels in the plywood, about 1¼ in. away from the edge of the block. Make a distinct, easily located mark on the block at the apex of the curve. When a hot, plasticized arm or bow is placed on the form for bending, its centerline should correspond to this mark. To complete the form, cut two ½-in.-thick dowels about 4 in. long, and make three hardwood wedges, 5 in. to 6 in. long. Taper the wedges from a cross section of about 1 in. square to a thin end.

Sack-Back Bending Form

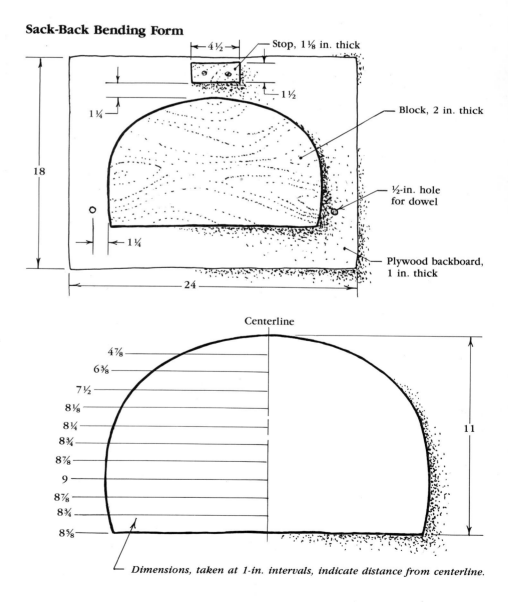

Dimensions, taken at 1-in. intervals, indicate distance from centerline.

19 *The continuous-arm bending form, clamped to a bench, ready for use.*

Continuous-Arm Bending Form

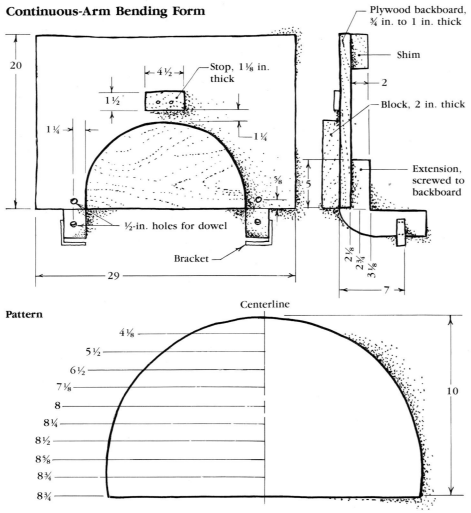

Dimensions, taken at 1-in. intervals, indicate distance from centerline.

The continuous-arm form This form has some similarities to the sack-back form (**19**). It, too, has a 2-in.-thick pine block attached to a plywood backboard. This block shapes the curve of the center segment of the continuous arm (the curve that will be in the vertical plane). Make a pattern to the curve shown on the drawing at left and cut the block to the curve. Nail the block flush with the edge of the plywood. At the top of the curve, screw a hardwood stop block to the plywood, 1¼ in. from the curve. Mark the center of the curve on the pine block.

This form has two extensions that are attached to the plywood. These shape the end segments of the continuous arm (they will be in the horizontal plane). I cut the extensions from 2-in.-thick pine. The drawing shows a pattern for the extensions, too. The top of each one is cut to a radius and notched to take the plywood backboard. Make sure that the radius will finish flush with the top surface of the plywood. Screw the extensions securely to the plywood.

20 *To bend a steamed sack-back arm, first align its center mark with that of the form. Wedge the arm between the hardwood stop block and the form.*

Bore ½-in. holes in the plywood near the base of the block or in each extension near the edge of the plywood and the outside surface of the extension. Dowels placed in these holes during bending hold the center segment in place on the form. The ends of the piece being bent are held down by two angled pieces of iron attached to the extensions. I use angle brackets available in any hardware store. You will also need two dowels and three wedges the same size as those for the sack-back bending form.

Bending the sack-back parts To use the steambox, fill the kettles with water up to the bottom of the spouts. (If this orifice is covered, the steam will escape around the kettle's lid, rather than rising through the spout into the pipe.) The pipe soon fills with a cloud of steam that cannot escape around the tight-fitting end caps. Its only egress is the small drain hole. When steam begins to blow out the hole in a plume that is 6 in. to 8 in. long, you are ready to insert the pieces. I will describe how to bend the sack-back parts first.

(In the photos, I am using a bending form made of a thin strip of wood attached to dowels. I made it about 12 years ago as an experiment, and have used it ever since. At the time, I thought it was a better solution to making a form than what I have just described, although it was so long ago that I have forgotten why. This form does not work any better or worse than one made of a solid block of wood, and it is more work to make.)

Place the arm and bow on the dowel rack and put the cap on the open end. The chamber is so tight that the parts will heat quickly. They will be ready in as little as 15 minutes, but I always give them more time. If the stock from which the backs are made has dried out, steam them for as much as 45 minutes to raise the moisture content back to 25%. While the parts are steaming, clamp the form securely to the bench.

Before removing a plasticized arm or bow from the steambox, I have one word of caution. When you open the pipe, the escaping steam can severely burn your skin. I was careless only once and lost the skin on my thumb because of a scald. When you take a part out of the pipe, do not do it with your bare hands. I prefer to seize the end of the part with a pair of pliers. Once the piece is safely away from the open end, I take it in my bare hands. I do not recommend wearing gloves because they

decrease sensitivity. Bending is not an exact science. It relies on intuition. You will need every possible bit of sensory data to achieve a successful bend. That data will be transmitted through sight, sound and feel. I would not wear gloves while bending any more than I would wear dark glasses.

If you look closely before pulling a part from the pipe, you might notice a curious phenomenon. The wood becomes so hot that sometimes the sap can be seen boiling out the end grain.

Pull a part out of the pipe with the pliers. Let's say it's the arm. The wood is so hot that you will have to pass it back and forth from hand to hand as you rush it to the bench. The discomfort is about as much as you can tolerate. It forces you to work quickly. And quickly you must. You have about 45 seconds in which to bend. By that time the piece will have cooled too much and will no longer be plastic.

Lay the arm between the pine block and the hardwood stop. Place one of the wide faces down and an edge against the pine block. Be careful to line up the center mark on the arm with the mark on the pine block that indicates the apex of the curve. Insert a wedge between the arm and the hardwood block, and give it a light rap with a hammer (**20**). This locks the wedge and tightly grips the arm against the pine block.

21 *Pull the first half around the form with a steady motion. When it is tight to the end of the form, insert a dowel into the backboard. Drive a wedge between the dowel and the arm so the dowel will not dimple the wood.*

Bend the first half of the arm by grasping it near the end with both hands and pulling with a steady motion (**21**). As I said earlier, bending is as much an intuition as a skill. It is very difficult to describe the process. As you bend the part, you can watch the wood move. The outside edge will stretch while the edge against the block compresses. Listen for any faint wrenching sounds that might indicate that the fibers are shearing either across or along the grain. Sometimes you can feel this shearing just as it begins to happen. If you hear or feel shearing, you may be pulling too fast for the wood to accept the stresses. Pull more slowly. On the other hand, if you pull too slowly, the part will cool and lose its plasticity before the bend is completed.

If a small shear does begin, you can sometimes push with one hand against the area that is shearing while continuing the bend with the other. Just that little bit of extra support may make the difference between losing the piece and saving it. For your first several bends, you might find it helpful to have an assistant help push where necessary.

The wood will only accept the bend if pulled with a steady, continuous motion. Do not jerk the end. When the first half is flush against the pine block, insert a dowel into the hole and slide a wedge between the dowel and the arm or bow. The wedge prevents the soft, hot wood from pressing against the dowel and developing a dimple.

The first half is always the easiest to bend. When the outside edge of the first half stretches, it steals some of its expansion from the outside edge of the other half. You can see this—the unbent half will move as the first bend is made. When you bend the second half, you will feel that it is stiffer. It has lost some flexibility to the first half, and the wood is cooler than it was during the first bend.

22 *Pull the second half of the arm around the form and hold it in place against the block with a dowel and wedge.*

23 *When the arm or bow is cool to the touch, tie its ends together with string. The part will retain the shape, and you can use the form to bend the next part.*

Pull the second half steadily, and a little slower than for the first half (**22**). Usually, if a part is going to break, it will do so during the second bend. Listen and feel for shearing and apply pressure to any suspect areas. When the second half is against the block, hold it in place with the same dowel and wedge arrangement used previously.

There is only one difference between bending an arm and a bow. A wide face of the arm must be placed down on the plywood backboard, and one edge against the pine block. The bow is round in cross section and has no distinct surface that must be placed against the block. Just remember to align the center marks of the bow and the block.

I usually make two chairs at a time. If I waited until an arm or bow was dry to take it off the form, I would need four bending jigs to make two sack backs. However, wood is only plastic when both heat and moisture are present. About 20 minutes after bending, the part will have cooled so that it is still wet, but no longer plastic. At this point I can tie its ends together to hold the curve, remove it from the form and bend the next arm or bow (**23**). Working this way, I can bend the arms and bows for a pair of sack-back chairs on one form in less than two hours.

In the winter, I hang the tied arms and bows over the stove in my shop to dry. In the summer, I set them outside in the sunshine. In a couple of days, when the chair backs are ready to assemble, I remove the string. The bent pieces will be dry enough to retain their shape permanently.

24 *Position the continuous arm face down on the backboard and wedge it in place.*

26 *Support the grain at the transition as you make the second bend.*

25 *Pull the first bend around the form and hold it in place with a wedge.*

Bending the continuous arm Pull the steamed arm from the pipe with pliers and place it face down on the form. Make sure that the inside edge (the straight edge, not the flared one) is against the block and the centerlines are aligned. Insert a wedge between the hardwood block and the arm (**24**). The first bend forms half of the curve of the center segment. It is made in exactly the same manner as the first bend of a sack-back arm or bow. Pull the arm steadily around the pine block and hold it in place against the block with a dowel and wedge (**25**).

The second bend is made downward over the curve of the form's extension. The short, tapered transition between the thick center segment and the thinner end segment will be at about the end of the pine block. Support the transition by pressing against it with one hand while bending with the other (**26**). The end grain exposed on the taper may lift loose rather than bend. This will happen to a certain extent every time that you bend a continuous arm. Pressing against the transition should keep the grain from lifting too much. The grain that does lift can be shaved away with a spokeshave after the part has dried.

There are four bends to be made in the continuous arm, and only about 45 seconds in which to make them. To save time, I usually hold the second bend in place with my knee, rather than taking the time to slip it under the angle bracket (**27**). I slip the two ends under the brackets after all the bends have been completed.

The second half of the arm will be stiffer than the first. Pull the third bend against the block and secure it with a dowel and wedge. Make the final bend while applying pressure to the area of the transition to prevent the grain from lifting (**28**). Finally, slip the second end, then the first, under the brackets.

27 *Hold the second bend in place with your knee while you make the remaining bends.*

28 *Bend the arm against the block, then over the extension (right). Then, slip both ends under the brackets (above).*

While the arm is wet and on the form, it is difficult to judge whether any torn or twisted grain that has occurred during bending will ruin it. (This is also true of the sack-back arm and bow.) When the arm has dried, you can examine it. Small flaws, such as a short section of wood that has sheared along the grain, can usually be trimmed flush to the surface with a spokeshave. Sheared grain up to ¼ in. thick can sometimes be glued and clamped back down in place. Of course, sometimes an arm cannot be saved. I do not lose many of them now, but when my bending intuition was still developing, the failure rate was much higher.

Because the continuous arm is bent in two planes, its ends cannot be tied so that it can be taken off the form. Still, I have not bothered to make two forms. I produce two of these chairs a week. I bend one arm on Monday and place it and the form near the stove or out in the sun, depending on the season. It will be dry by Wednesday and can be removed to free the form for the second arm. This arm will be dry by Friday, when I put the chairs together.

29 *To make hands for either chair, joint the mating edges of the blocks and the arm (top). Size the edges, then glue and clamp the pieces together. Here, a vise serves as a clamp (bottom).*

30 *Plane the blocks flush with the arm after the glue has dried.*

Finishing Up

When the bent parts are dry, they are in no condition to be used on the chair. The hands need to be made and the rough surfaces smoothed. The hands of a Windsor are at the ends of its arm, where the sitter places his hands. Hands are generally any one of a number of scrolled shapes. The hands of the sack back and continuous arm are wider than the ends of the arms, so pieces have to be glued on to form them.

There are several reasons why these pieces are glued on to make the hands, rather than making them from the same piece of wood as the arm. To get the wider hand out of one piece, you would have to start with a larger blank. This means more work and more waste. If the arm breaks while being bent, the work that goes into making the hand is lost. To shape the hand from one piece, you would have to saw into the back edge of the arm. This sawing would actually increase the odds of the arm breaking during bending.

There is another consideration for the sack back. Its scrolled hand has delicate details. If cut in oak or some other ring-porous wood suitable for bending, these details would be very fragile. A blow to the middle of the hand could easily break the point off.

To overcome these problems, I glue pieces of birch to the edges of the arm after bending. I prefer birch because it is less fragile than oak and finishes smoothly even on end grain. It planes and saws well, and it is easy to clean up the edges of the scroll with a chisel after the shape has been cut out. There are always a lot of birch scraps from turning stock lying around the shop. I split these into short blocks about 1 in. thick, 6 in. long and 2 in. wide, and then set them aside to dry. If the birch blocks are the same thickness as the arm before gluing up, you will have a devil of a time aligning the surfaces. It is a lot easier to glue on a block that is thicker than the arm and then plane the surfaces flush.

31 *To shape a continuous-arm hand, angle the coping saw as you cut to produce a beveled edge. Clean up with a spokeshave, working with the grain.*

32 *Cut the scroll of the sack-back hand perpendicular to the faces of the arm. The concave curve of the scroll is best cleaned up with a gouge.*

The hands of a Windsor endure a lot of stress and strain. People are forever putting their weight on them as they get in and out of the chair. It is essential that the joint of a block to the arm not fail. A good joint requires perfectly mated edges. It would be dangerous to joint these edges on a machine jointer. So, I clamp my jointer plane upside down in a vise and run the edges over it (**29**). The resulting surfaces are as good as any done mechanically.

As insurance for a good joint, I always size the mating edges before gluing and clamping. Sizing is done by wiping a thin film of glue over each edge and allowing it to dry. When the joint is ready to be assembled, a second layer of glue is applied. The first application prevents the second from being forced into the wood by the pressure of the clamps.

After the glue has dried, clamp the arm to the bench and plane the block flush with the arm (**30**). Next, trace the pattern onto the hand and saw out the shape with a coping saw. The edge of the scroll on the sack-back hand is at a right angle to the upper surface of the arm. The edge of the hand for the continuous arm is cut at a bevel (**31**). I clean up the saw marks on the sack-back hand with a chisel and a gouge that fits the curve of the scroll (**32**). On the continuous arm, the cleanup can be done with a spokeshave.

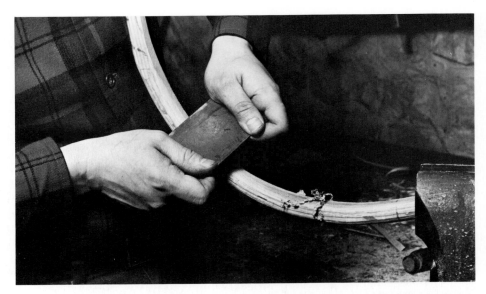

33 *Clean up the rough surfaces on a continuous arm and the sack-back arm and bow with a cabinet scraper. A curved block will help hold the bent parts in a vise for scraping.*

The hands are finished, but the rest of the bent part remains rough. I secure the part in my tin-knocker's vise and clean it up with a cabinet scraper (**33**). A curved block of wood helps hold the curves of the parts in place in the vise. The scraper removes the grain raised by steaming, and it also eliminates any remaining tool marks. Purple spots that result from the tannic acid in the oak coming in contact with ferrous metal can be scraped off as well. A light sanding with 220-grit paper is all that is required to finish the surfaces. The arm and bow for the sack back and the continuous arm are all scraped and sanded in the same way.

My continuous arm has a bead molding on the top and bottom arrises of the face. This molding could have been worked on the arm before it was bent. I did not do it then because the work would have been wasted if the part did not survive bending. Instead, I work the molding after scraping the arm (**34**). I made a simple scratch tool for this. The scratch appears primitive, but its cutting action is really rather complicated. To make the tool, cut a small hardwood block about 1 in. by ¾ in. by 3½ in. Drive a 1-in. No. 10 or No. 12 flat-head wood screw into the 1-in.-wide face about ⅞ in. from the end. Gently round the face from which the head of the screw protrudes. This will allow the tool to track on even very tight curves.

34 *Make a simple scratch tool for beading the continuous arm from a small hardwood block and a flat-head screw (right). Push the block against the edges of the arm and draw the screw over the face until a groove is formed. Round the arrises to form a bead.*

The edge of the slot in the screw head cuts the groove that forms the bead. The slot acts like the throat in a molding plane. A thin chip curls upward as the groove is formed. Acting as a fence, the hardwood block maintains the cut at a uniform distance from the edge of the arm. You can vary the width of the bead by either backing out the screw or advancing it. After scratching the grooves, round the arrises with a cabinet scraper to produce the beads.

Hang the bent part or parts out of the way until after you have whittled the spindles and are ready to assemble the chair back.

Chapter VII

Whittling the Spindles

The following conversation is typical of many I have had when introduced to a new acquaintance:

"What line of work are you in?"

"I make Windsor chairs."

"Windsors, aren't those the ones with all the spokes at the back?"

It is not surprising that this is the recollection most people have of Windsors. The image they retain is of only the most dominant features, and the spindles in the back of a Windsor create a very strong impression. They are pronounced verticals that seize the viewer's attention and draw it upward in the direction of their flare. The role of spindles in the engineering of a Windsor-chair back is equally important. They act as thin, vertical springs, absorbing the weight of a sitter rather than resisting it. Thus, the spindles allow the back of a Windsor to be delicate and airy without being fragile.

It is extremely important to the longevity of the chair that the spindles be capable of flexing without breaking. The only way to ensure this is to make them from riven wood. At no point along the spindle's shaft should the grain run out. If it does, the spindle will be severely weakened. The stock for spindles of modern, factory-made Windsors is sawn into squares. The saw is oblivious to the direction of the grain and cuts across it as easily as along it. To ensure sufficient strength, therefore, factory-made spindles must be thicker than handmade, riven spindles.

Wood for making spindles should have the same qualities as wood for bending, as described in Chapter VI. It must be flexible and easily worked. It must also split well. I use red oak for spindles because I always have plenty of it on hand. Unseasoned hickory or white ash are equally good. You need not be concerned about the hardness that develops in ash or hickory as they season, because no holes are bored in a spindle. I still recommend against white oak, because it does not usually rive cleanly. However, if it is the only available wood, it will be adequate.

Riving The longest spindle blank that you will need for either chair is 22 in., so first buck a 22-in. length of oak from a log. I halve and quarter this on the spot, then bring the smaller, more transportable billets into the shop. Remove the bark from the quarters with a drawknife, then place them on a chopping block and rive them with a hatchet and maul. Be careful to split pieces of equal mass, and reduce the quarters to as many spindle blanks as you need (1). The cross section of each blank should be about 1 in. square.

1 *Split 1-in.-square spindle blanks with a hatchet and maul. Be sure to plan the riving sequence so you are always splitting pieces of equal mass.*

The continuous-arm chair requires eleven whittled spindles, the sack-back chair seven. Even red oak requires more effort to work as it becomes drier, so I split only enough spindle blanks for the two chairs that I make in a week. Working freshly split wood saves wear and tear on my tools and myself. However, if a billet renders more blanks than I need, I am not about to discard good wood—I set the extras aside and use them the following week.

I whittle my spindles with a draw-knife and spokeshave. I hold the end of the blank securely in my tin-knocker's vise. I much prefer this vise to a shave horse. Held in the vise, the blank projects into my work area and is accessible from three directions: the top and both sides. On a shave horse, I cannot work as much surface area, so the spindle needs to be continually released and moved to whittle all surfaces. Using my tin-knocker's vise, I need to move the spindle fewer times.

The spindles for the two chairs look much the same, but there are a few differences in the way they are made. I will first discuss continuous-arm spindles, which are simpler to make.

2 *Rough-out the long, thin end of the spindle with a drawknife.*

3 *Work the last 6 in. or so of the bottom end with the drawknife. Turn the spindle again and thin the shaft above the swelling.*

Continuous-arm spindles First, cut the eleven spindle blanks to length. Blanks for the three center spindles and two brace spindles should be 22 in. long. Cut two more blanks 21 in. long, two blanks 19 in. long and a final pair 17 in. long. All of these lengths are longer than the visible shaft of the spindle. The extra length allows for a 1¼-in. tenon at the bottom end and a tenon of about ⅞ in. at the top, which fits into a socket in the arm. The rest of the extra length is waste, but it is necessary for assembling the back.

Grasp the bottom end of the blank in a vise. First, rough-out the thinner, top part with a drawknife. I start my cuts about three fifths of the way down the shaft (**2**). When this end has its basic shape, turn the blank around and work the other, thicker end (**3**). Drawknife up from the end only about 6 in. This leaves a definite swelling below the center of the roughed-out shaft. Turn the spindle again and work the long shaft above the swelling.

The swelling is very important. The back of a Windsor should be light and airy. However, as is true of most of the other design considerations, there can be too much of a good thing. The spindles would look like wires if they were uninterrupted tapers from the ⁹⁄₁₆-in. socket in the seat to the ⅜-in. socket in the arm. The back would look fragile. The spindles flare out from the seat, but because of the swelling in each one, there is no real increase in the distance between them for the first two fifths of their length. The spindles appear to

4 *After drawknifing the spindle roughly to shape, switch to a spokeshave. Rotate the spindle frequently so you maintain its round cross section.*

5 *The ends of a spindle fit into sockets in the seat and arm. Check their thicknesses with a simple wooden gauge as you work. The top end of a spindle should pass through a hole ⅜ in. in diameter, as shown here, the bottom end through a hole ⅝ in. in diameter.*

spread only above the level of the arms. The long, thin portions of the spindles create an open, delicate fan, while the swellings restrain this effect.

Next, smooth the roughly shaped spindle with a spokeshave (**4**). Because the wood was riven, the grain runs only in one direction. The spokeshave will remove long, thin shavings. This work is easy, and my only caution is to not get carried away with it. Be sure to rotate the spindle occasionally and to work all the sides. The tendency for a beginner is to work one area for too long. This results in spindles that are oval in cross section.

The ends of each spindle will be socketed into the seat and the arm, and must fit snugly. I gauge the size of the ends by eye while spokeshaving. Until you have more experience and feel confident gauging by eye, you may want to use a simple gauge made from scrap wood. Bore a hole in the scrap with the same bit you will use to bore the spindle sockets in the arm—I use my ⅜-in. spoon bit. Gauge the thickness of the spindle's top end with this hole (**5**).

6 *Blend the swelling into the rest of the shaft, but don't lose it. To keep the thin, flexible shaft still while spokeshaving, you can support the free end against your stomach.*

Bore a second hole for gauging the bottom ends of the spindles. When assembling the chair, you will whittle a shouldered tenon on the bottom of each spindle. So for now, you will want these ends to pass through a hole slightly larger than the sockets. The spindle sockets are ⁹⁄₁₆ in. in diameter, so the last 1¼ in. or so of each spindle should fit snugly in a ⅝-in. hole.

Finally, blend the swelling into the shaft above and below it (6). The diameter of the swelling on my spindles is about ⅝ in. to ¾ in. However, in both the sack back and the continuous arm, the area of the back where the swellings line up is so busy that the eye cannot detect slight variations in them. Because the diameter of the swelling is not critical, do not bother to check it with a gauge. Make sure, however, that the swellings are not too pronounced. The vertical lines of the spindles draw the eye up to the curve of the arm; if the swellings are too heavy, this upward motion is disturbed.

Sack-back spindles The seven sack-back spindles are made in almost the same way as the continuous-arm spindles. The sack-back spindles, however, have to pass through the arm before being wedged into the through sockets in the bow. The joints at the arm cannot be wedged, so they must be a tight friction-fit. The arm ties the spindles together and strengthens them, but if the spindles are loose in the arm sockets, these functions are subverted. Therefore, the diameter of each spindle where it passes through the arm socket is critical.

You will need to gauge the spindles to ensure a tight fit. The sockets in the arm and bow are bored with a ⅜-in. spoon bit. To make the gauge, bore a hole with that bit in a piece of scrap hardwood. In the time it takes to make and assemble the back, spindles made of freshly riven wood will shrink. To allow for this shrinkage, I enlarge the ⅜-in. hole about ¹⁄₃₂ in. with a rat-tail file. I do occasionally use blanks left over from the previous week's chairs. In the winter, these blanks will have dried

considerably and will not shrink as much as a freshly riven blank. I fit spindles made of dry wood to the gauge; these, and any others that do not fit properly, will be spokeshaved or scraped to fit during the dry assembly of the back.

The spindles must also tighten in the arm at a predetermined height. If a spindle tightens too high up its length, the distance between the arm and the seat will be too great. This would make it impossible to assemble the back. If the spindle tightens too low on the shaft, the joint will be loose. You need another gauge to ensure that the shaft is a tight fit at the correct height. The bottom of the arm should be about 8½ in. to 8¾ in. above the surface of the seat, and the bottom tenon of each spindle is 1¼ in. long, so cut a stick about 10 in. long for the gauge.

7 Sack-back spindles are made in the same way as those for the continuous-arm chair. However, they must fit tightly where they pass through the arm. Make two gauges to ensure that the spindles are the correct diameter at the correct height.

8 After the spindles have dried, remove stains and whittling marks with a cabinet scraper.

To make the spindles, cut three blanks 22 in. long, two 21 in. long and the remaining pair 19 in. long. Rough-out and do the initial spokeshaving of each spindle as described earlier. As you approach the correct diameter at the top end of the spindle, slip the diameter gauge over the top end. As you work the gauge down the shaft of the spindle, it finds the high spots and shows you how much more wood to shave away. As the gauge approaches the middle of the spindle's length, check its distance from the lower end with the length gauge. Keep shaving, and when the two gauges meet, about 10 in. from the spindle's bottom end, it is time to stop (7).

Turn the spindle around once again and finish its lower end. Then complete the swelling, as described earlier. The diameters of each spindle at its top and bottom are also ⅜ in. and ⅝ in., respectively. I recommend a gauge like the one described for the continuous-arm chair to check the bottom end.

When all the spindles are whittled, place them aside to dry. In the winter, I suspend them over the wood stove in my shop. In the summer, I set them out with the bent parts in the sun. In damp weather, you can dry them in the oven, like the armposts, short spindles and center stretcher. When dry, the spindles scrape very well. I remove all the whittling marks and any stains with a cabinet scraper (8). A light sanding with 220-grit sandpaper finishes them.

Spindles are the easiest parts of the chair to make. I do a lot of daydreaming when making them. Spindles for a continuous arm require about three minutes apiece, those for a sack back about five minutes, so it takes me a little over an hour to make spindles for a pair of either type of chair.

At some point, you will probably be tempted to try to make spindles on the lathe. However, you will quickly become so frustrated that you will return to whittling them. Spindles are too long and thin to turn unless you are very experienced and use a steady rest.

If you want to use a lathe, it is feasible to turn the lower part of the spindle, including the shouldered tenon and the swelling. However, the more flexible, upper length will still have to be whittled. There are some problems with this technique: The turned and whittled segments must be blended together with a spokeshave. Some vibration will still occur in the lathe, so the surface of the swelling will contain some nicks that must also be removed with the shave. The cleanup needed with this method exceeds the labor required to whittle the spindles in the first place.

Chapter VIII

Assembling the Sack Back

Whittling the spindles completes the making of parts for the chair back, and now you are ready to assemble it. The order in which several of the initial steps are done can vary. I will begin here by boring the armpost sockets in the arm, then boring the spindle sockets in the seat. You could reverse this order, as I do in the following chapter when assembling the continuous arm.

Armpost sockets Insert the armposts in the seat and place the arm on top of the tenons. Stand behind the chair and hold the arm roughly parallel to the plane of the seat. Position the hands so they intersect the armposts approximately where the sockets should be. On my chairs, this is about 2 in. from the end of either hand. Sight down from above to see how the arm relates to the curvature of the spindle-socket positions marked on the seat. The two curves are not identical, so try to position them symmetrically.

When you are satisfied with the position of the arm, mark where one post would intersect the top surface of a hand (**1**). Because the armpost will pierce the hand at an angle, make sure to place the socket so that it will not be too close to the inside edge of the hand and weaken it. To bore the socket, clamp the arm and a backing board to the benchtop. The hole is bored from the top surface, for the same reasons that the seat sockets are bored from the top of the seat (p. 47). Clamp near the hand, being sure to leave enough space to turn the brace without striking the clamp. Before boring the hole, I return to the chair and sight down the post, mentally checking its slope and flare angles. They must be reproduced in the socket. I suggest that for your first chair, you set bevel squares to these angles and check the brace against them as you bore the socket.

Start the $7/16$-in. spoon bit at a right angle to the hand, then lower it into position as you turn the brace (**2**). When you bore this hole, do not bore as fast as the spoon bit will allow. The arm is narrow and could split if you press too hard on the brace and bit.

The armpost tenon is tapered, so the socket must be reamed. Grip the hand in a vise, bottom surface toward you. The arm is quite thin in comparison to the seat, so ream slowly, allowing the tool to enter the socket at its own pace (**3**). Periodically, remove the reamer and test-fit the corresponding armpost tenon. When the tenon can be inserted so that only the large end of its taper is exposed beneath the arm, the socket is complete. (You might want to bore and ream a socket in a piece of $7/16$-in.-thick scrap wood for practice before trying one in the arm.)

1 *Position the arm on the armposts and mark one socket on a hand.*

2 *Bore the first socket carefully; check the angles against bevel squares if necessary.*

3 *Ream the socket so that the tenon fits into it up to the base of the taper.*

4 *Put the first socket over its armpost, and position the arm for marking the second socket. The arm and the spindle-socket marks should form symmetrical arcs.*

Return to the seat and slip the socket over the armpost tenon. The arm will rotate on this single point. Rest the un-socketed hand on the other post. Stand behind the chair again and adjust the arm so that it is symmetrical with the spindle-socket marks. You should see something like what is shown in photo **4**. Make sure that the position of the hand on the post is correct, then mark the second socket. (This certainty of adjustment was not possible before boring the first socket.) Clamp the arm to the bench, establish the brace at the correct angles and bore the second socket. Ream and fit it to the armpost tenon.

Slip the arm over both armpost tenons, then stand back to examine the chair from a distance. The arm should be nearly parallel to the plane of the seat. You needn't worry if the seat and arm converge slightly, but if they diverge, you may have to correct the angles of the armpost sockets in the arm. Test how much the arm will flex; if the error is small, you should be able to pull it down until it is parallel to the seat. If the error is large, use the reamer to adjust the angles, but be careful not to enlarge the sockets too much.

When you are satisfied with the relationship of the arm to the seat, measure the height of the hands from the seat on both sides. If there is any discrepancy between them, ream the socket on the higher side again. Before proceeding further, swap the posts to see if they are interchangeable. If not, mark them left and right.

5 *Bore the socket for the center spindle first. Viewed from the front, it is perpendicular to the seat.*

Spindle sockets in the seat As I mentioned in Chapter IV, the beginner should bore the spindle sockets in the seat now, rather than when socketing the seat for the armposts and legs. By placing the arm on the armposts, you can get a sense of what the spindle flare and slope angles should be. Then, with the chair resting on the floor, you can sight down the brace, very much like what would be done when aiming a rifle, to establish these angles when boring each socket.

At first, you will probably want to check the brace and bit with bevel squares. (Approximate angles are given on the drawing at right.) As you gain experience, you will not need the bevel squares. Eventually, you will remember these angles so well that you will be able to bore all the sockets in the seat at the same time. I find this the most efficient method.

Spindle Angles for Sack Back

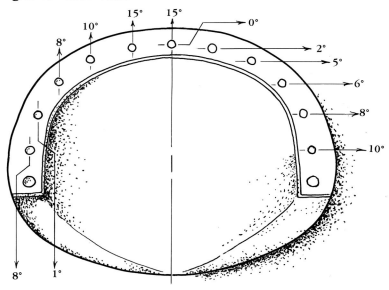

Slope is indicated on the left half of the drawing. Flare is shown on the right. Arrows indicate direction of slope or flare. The spindles are symmetrical around the center spindle.

6 *You can sight down the brace and bit to establish the slope and flare angles for the remaining spindle sockets. The axis of the brace and bit should correspond to the position of the spindle. You can use bevel squares to check the angles until you gain confidence in sighting.*

7 *Trim the spindle tenons to fit the sockets. Facet the tenons with a wide, shallow gouge or chisel. The facets will bite into the socket walls so the tenon will not twist.*

I bore the sockets with a ⁹⁄₁₆-in. spoon bit that has a scribe mark 1¼ in. from its nose. This mark indicates when the socket is deep enough. Bore the socket for the center spindle first. This spindle slopes back, but it is perpendicular to the seat when viewed from the front. You could say that it has zero flare. You can use a try square to establish this angle, or gauge it by eye (**5**).

The remaining spindles have both slope and flare. Corresponding spindles on either side of the center are mirror images. I bore one of the sockets adjacent to the center spindle, then the adjacent socket on the other side. I repeat this process for each pair. This helps because I have the slope and flare of the first spindle in mind and need only reverse the direction of the flare for the second (**6**). If you are checking the angles with bevel squares, you can use the same settings for each pair of spindles.

When all the sockets are bored in the seat, I like to whittle the tenons on the ends of the long spindles and insert them in the appropriate holes. I whittle the tenons by holding a wide, shallow carving gouge against my sternum and pulling the tenon against it (**7**). The tenons should be about 1¼ in. long. They should fit the sockets tightly and have pronounced facets. These facets key the joint, much like the oversized wedges do for the leg tenons. The facets bite into the walls of the sockets, minimizing the ability of the spindle to twist. You do not need to round the bottoms of the tenons to conform to the socket bottoms—the hard, oak tenon will make the socket conform to it. At the same time, shave the egg-shaped tenons of the short spindles to fit their seat sockets.

When all the spindles are in place, step back to view the chair. You can now spot any discrepancies in the angles of the spindles. The spindles are flexible and consequently very forgiving of error. If one appears incorrect, see if you can pull it into place. If it is too far out of kilter, you can adjust the flare of the surrounding spindles when you bore the sockets in the arm and bow, so that the spindles appear even and symmetrical. At the worst, you might have to plug the socket in the seat and bore a new one.

At this time, you will notice that the project is beginning to look like a chair. Even after all the Windsors I have made, I still appreciate this moment, and I find it a satisfying time to take a coffee break.

9 *Check the socket locations on the arm against the spindles. Small adjustments to align a spindle and a socket will not be noticeable.*

8 *Mark the position of the socket for the center spindle on the arm. Then walk off the remaining sockets with a pair of dividers.*

Spindle sockets in the arm With the arm attached to the two posts, place the center spindle in its socket. It should rest against the arm at the middle of the curve. However, bent wood is never perfectly symmetrical. Some adjustment of the spindle from side to side may be necessary. A couple of degrees of movement either way is possible without being obvious.

When you are satisfied with the position, mark the intersection of the spindle and the arm. Next, set a pair of dividers and walk off the sockets for the remaining spindles (**8**). On my sack backs, there is 2⅞ in. between all the long spindles. When the positions are marked, insert all the spindles in the seat and check them against the socket locations on the arm (**9**). This is the time to adjust for any discrepancy in the flare of the spindles.

Locate the sockets in the arm for the short spindles by eye, rather than with dividers. Because the arm is not symmetrical, it may not be the same length on both sides of the center spindle. You can hide this discrepancy by locating the short-spindle sockets so that they divide the length of arm between the outside long spindle and the armpost socket into three equal sections (**10**).

10 *Locate the sockets for the short spindles by eye. The sockets should divide the distance between the outside long spindle and the armpost socket into three equal sections.*

11 *Bore the center-spindle socket in the arm, then corresponding sockets on either side of the center. Judge the slope and flare angles by eye, or with bevel squares.*

To bore the sockets in the arm, clamp it to the bench over a backing board to prevent break-out. I make the long-spindle sockets with a ⅜-in. spoon bit, the short-spindle sockets with a ⁷⁄₁₆-in. bit. A small *C*-clamp will prevent the bit from splitting the arm. This sort of accident does not happen often, but when it does, it is doubly aggravating—first, because it happened at all, and second, because a little foresight could have prevented it.

I usually start with the center spindle socket (**11**), then I bore pairs of sockets on either side of the center, as described earlier. Remember to position the socket toward the outside edge of the arm, so that the angled hole will not weaken the inside edge.

I bore these sockets by eye, but if you are hesitant to try this, use bevel squares set to the same angles as the spindle sockets in the seat. If you decide to try it by eye, here's a word of caution: The slope and flare angles for the long spindles are not extreme, and a beginner will usually exaggerate them. It is difficult to see such a slight angle when sighting down the brace from above. Try holding the brace at the correct angles with one hand while you squat down behind it to check the flare, then move to the side to check the slope. The flexibility of the spindles will forgive a certain amount of error in boring these sockets.

12 *Insert the spindles in their arm sockets, and check that they extend the correct distance below the arm.*

13 *Dry-fit the spindles and arm. Tap the spindle tenons part of the way into the seat sockets.*

Assembling the lower back When all the sockets are bored in the arm, dry-assemble the lower back (the spindles, arm and armposts). First, put the long and short spindles in their arm sockets. Check the long spindles with a tape measure (or the length gauge that you used when whittling them) to make sure that they extend about 10 in. below the arm (**12**). This will ensure that the arm will rest at the correct height on the spindles when the back is assembled. Scrape or shave any spindles that are too thick until they fit correctly.

With all the spindles in their arm sockets, place the arm on the armpost tenons. Tap the spindles down one by one until their tenons have begun to enter the seat sockets (**13**). You only want to test the fit of the back now, so do not drive the tenons home. You want the tenon facets to bite fully into the socket walls only at final assembly. Next, tap the arm down into place on the spindles.

I like the arm to sit about ½ in. lower at the center of the back than at the armposts. This slight drop counters an undesirable optical illusion—when the arm and the seat are parallel, the arm appears to be higher at the back than at the posts. By dropping the arm at the rear, you create the illusion that it is parallel with the seat. When the back is finally assembled, the distance from the top surface of the arm to the seat at the center spindle should be about 9 in.; at the armposts, it should be about 9 ½ in. (When measuring at dry-assembly, remember to allow for the amount that the tenons will be driven in at final assembly.) These heights can vary from chair to chair, because the lengths of the tenons or the size of the reamed sockets for the armposts may be different on one chair than on another.

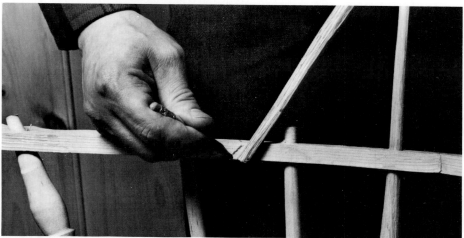

14 *Weave the bow through the long spindles of the dry-assembled chair (top left). Adjust its position, then mark the location of the sockets on the arm. Indicate the slope angle of the bow on the inside edge of the arm (bottom left).*

15 *To bore the sockets for the bow, start the bit perpendicular to the arm (bottom right) and gradually lower it to the slope angle drawn on the arm (top right).*

Before gluing up the lower back, you need to bore the sockets that join the bow to the arm. Put the bow in place on the dry-assembled chair. Weave the bow through the spindles, one spindle to one side of the bow, the next to the other side, and so on (**14**). This holds the bow in the plane it will occupy when the chair is finally assembled. If the bow were merely rested against the fronts of the spindles, it would be too far forward. Behind them, it would be too far back.

Roughly locate the ends of the bow between the two short spindles. Look down on the bow from behind and adjust it so it is symmetrical in relation to the curve of the seat and the curve of the arm. When you are satisfied with the position, mark the location of both sockets on the top surface of the arm. The bow slopes back, but has no flare, so you can center the sockets on the arm. The ends of the bow cross the arm at the angle of the sockets. Trace this angle on the inside edge of the arm to serve as a guide when you are boring the socket.

Remove the arm by tapping it off the spindles with a hammer. Strike between all the spindles, alternating the hammer blows to raise the arm evenly and prevent it from binding. If the arm catches on one of the spindles, the thin walls of the socket could break.

Clamp the arm and a backing board to the benchtop so that you can see the angled scribe mark on the inside edge of the arm. I lay the hand parallel to the edge of the benchtop. Put a small C-clamp on the arm to prevent the bit from splitting it while you bore the socket. Make sure that the clamp does not cover the angled scribe mark. Start the ⅜-in. spoon bit at a right angle, then gradually lower it to match the angled mark and complete the socket (**15**). Bore the sockets for both ends of the bow in this way.

16 *During final assembly, drive the spindles into the seat sockets. Then tap between the spindles to set the arm in position, alternating blows from side to side. Measure from the seat to check the arm's height at the center spindle and armposts.*

17 *Wedge the short spindles and armposts in the arm. Make the split for the wedge at a right angle to the grain of the arm.*

There is an alternate method that a beginner might feel more comfortable with. In this method, the sockets for the bow are bored after the lower back (the spindles, arm and armposts) has been glued in place. Go through basically the same procedure as just described. The sockets, however, are made with a ratchet brace while the arm is fixed to the chair. Be sure to use a C-clamp here as well, to prevent splitting.

When the sockets for the bow have been bored, the lower back is ready for the final assembly. I recommend assembling in the following order to minimize glue spillage and the resulting mess. First, put all the long spindles in the proper arm sockets. Do not glue these joints—glue only bonds well under pressure, and there is no way to wedge these joints.

Next, swab glue into all the spindle sockets in the seat, then put glue into the four short-spindle sockets in the arm and insert the short spindles. Spread glue on the walls of the armpost sockets in the seat and insert the armposts. (Remember to put them in their proper sockets if they have been marked left and right.) Finally, put glue in the armpost sockets in the arm, and set the arm down onto the posts.

Line each spindle up with its seat socket, and tap the tenon in. When all the tenons are in the sockets, give each spindle a firm rap to set the tenon facets into the soft, pine sides of the sockets. Now, tap the arm down to correct height (½ in. lower at the back than at the armposts), and measure to check (**16**). Be sure not to cock the arm on the spindles by driving it in only one area. Tap around the whole arc, working the arm down uniformly. Do not drive the arm down too aggressively. Also, remember that the tapered tenons on both ends of the armposts can act as wedges and can split the seat or arm if driven with too much force.

18 *Rest the arm on a benchtop and wedge the armpost tenons into the seat.*

19 *Shave the tenons and wedges flush with the arm, then scrape and sand the surfaces.*

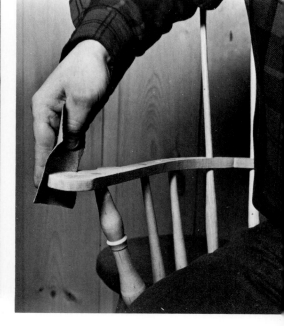

When the arm is at the desired height, trim the tops of the short spindles and the armpost tenons with a coping saw so that no more than ¼ in. is left above the arm. These parts are smeared with glue, and when the teeth of the coping-saw blade become clogged, the blade can be disposed of. Wedge these tenons in the same manner as the leg tenons (**17**). I shape the wedges with a drawknife or a wide, shallow gouge, depending on how much wood must be removed. Do not make the wedges wider than the tenons. The arm is thinner than the seat and made of hardwood, so instead of keying the joint, an overwide wedge could split the arm. Make the slots with a chisel in the end grain of the tenons. When driving the wedges, listen for the dull tone that indicates when to stop.

After wedging the joints in the arm, invert the chair on a benchtop and wedge the posts into the seat (**18**). Do not key this wedge either—the distance between the socket and the edge of the seat is short, and too much pressure could cause a crack to open in the end grain of the seat. Set the chair upright and shave the protruding tenons and wedges flush with the arm (**19**). I do this with the wide, shallow gouge that I use for making wedges and whittling tenons. Then scrape the arm with a cabinet scraper and lightly sand it with 220-grit sandpaper.

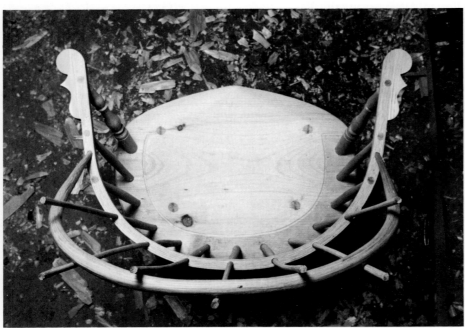

20 *Weave the bow through the spindles and adjust its position. The bow should be symmetrical to the curves of the arm and seat.*

21 *Brace the chair against the bench and support the bow with your knee while boring the socket for the center spindle. Sight down the brace to establish the slope and flare angles.*

Spindle sockets in the bow Shave the ends of the bow with a spokeshave until they fit into a ⅜-in. hole bored in a gauge block. Then, weave the bow through the spindles and insert the ends of the bow into the sockets in the arm. The center spindle should now cross the bow at the location of its socket. While the spindles hold the bow in place, step in front of the chair and make sure that you are satisfied with the location of the center spindle. Some adjustment may be necessary to center the spindle and ensure that the bow is symmetrical (**20**). If, when adjusting the bow, an end hits a short spindle, just remove the bow and trim the end.

Mark the socket for the center spindle. With the brace and bit at the ready, place your toe on the back of the seat behind the spindles and support the bow with your knee (**21**). Keep the chair from moving by pushing it against a workbench or wall.

Boring this socket is a delicate operation, but your knee should give you all the support you need to prevent shearing the ends of the bow at the arm. Bore gently and slowly, sighting down the axis of the brace and bit as you would down the barrel of a rifle. Aim at the spindle's arm socket. This should also line up in your sight with the spindle's seat socket.

It is difficult and unnecessary to attach a waste block to the bow to prevent break-out. The bow is round in cross section, so when the spoon bit exits, a burr is created, rather than splinters. I remove the burr with the wide, shallow gouge. If any more break-out occurs, it will not be visible because it will be on the underside of the bow.

22 *Insert the center spindle in its socket, and reposition the bow. Then walk off the positions of the two adjacent sockets with dividers and bore the holes.*

23 *Start the sockets for the fourth and fifth spindles perpendicular to the bow (left). Sight down the brace and gradually move the bit to the correct angle (above).*

Once the socket is complete, pull the ends of the bow out of the arm and insert the end of the center spindle in the socket. Weave the bow through the other spindles for support and put the ends back in the arm sockets. With a pair of dividers, walk off the positions of the two sockets adjacent to the center spindle (**22**). (I set the dividers from my model chair; you can take these measurements from the drawing on p. 131. Remember that your chair may differ from these approximate measurements. You may need to adjust the position of the sockets in the bow slightly to align them with those in the arm and seat.) When the sockets are satisfactorily marked, place your knee against the bow and bore each hole. Repeat the process for the next two spindles. Remember to start the bit perpendicular to the bow, and gradually move it to the correct angle. Sight down the brace as before to establish this angle (**23**).

25 *Whittle a point on each outside spindle to make assembly easier.*

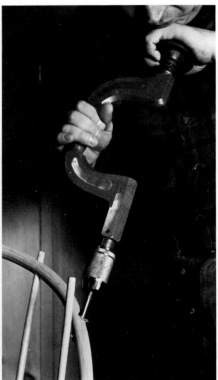

24 *The final two spindle sockets are the riskiest. Start the bit at a right angle to the bow. Bore slowly and raise the brace to the correct angle as the hole deepens.*

When the bow is set over these five spindles, it will be well enough supported so that you will not need to use your knee when boring the remaining two sockets. It is just as well. Boring these sockets is riskier than anything you have done so far. They intersect the bow at such an extreme angle that I know of no bit other than a spoon bit that I would trust to make them.

Mark the location of these outside sockets with the dividers. Start the bit at a right angle to the surface of the bow (**24**). The bit will be almost parallel to the plane of the seat. As you deepen the hole, sight down the brace and slowly bring the bit up to the correct slope and flare angles. Finish the hole gently—at this angle, the burr on the underside of the bow can be heavy.

When the last two sockets have been bored in the bow, whittle a point on the ends of the last two spindles—they should look like sharpened pencils (**25**). When the sharpened ends are driven through their sockets, they will not catch on the socket walls and plow a piece of the bow out in front of them. Remove the bow, then trim and sand the burr off the underside of each socket. I do not recommend dry-assembling the parts, because piloting the two outside spindles into their sockets is so difficult that I do not like to do it twice. Also, there is very little that could go wrong during final assembly, because you will have already tested five of the seven spindles in their sockets.

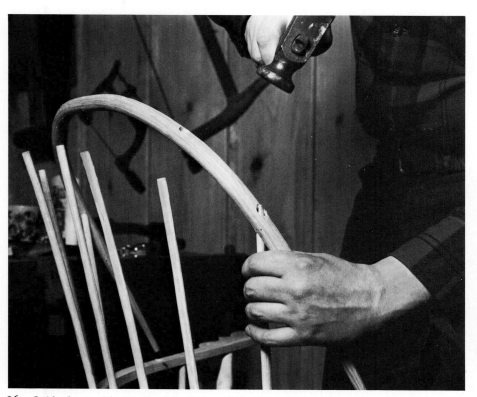

26 *Guide the outside spindles into their sockets, then tap near the sockets to begin lowering the bow.*

27 *When all the spindles and the ends of the bow are in their sockets, tap the bow into alignment so that it is symmetrical around the center spindle and of equal height on both sides.*

Assembling the upper back You are now ready to mount the bow on the back. Begin by smearing glue in all the bow's spindle sockets, and the two sockets for the bow in the arm. Hold the bow above the spindles and set the top ends of the two outside spindles in their sockets (**26**). Tap with a hammer next to these two sockets to begin lowering the bow. Throughout the process of driving the bow onto the spindles, be sure to alternate your hammer blows from side to side, working along the length of the bow. If you drive one side too far, the bow might catch on a spindle. Because the bow will not be able to move at this point, it will rack and could break at the hung-up socket.

As the bow lowers, two more spindles will line up with their sockets, and you can guide them in. The ends of the bow may contact the arm now also, so insert them in their sockets. Continue to tap from side to side on the bow as you line up and insert the last three spindles in their sockets.

With the bow mounted, turn your attention to aligning it on the chair. The center spindle should appear to bisect the area encompassed by the bow. The bow should not be higher on one side of the center spindle than the other. If it is, tap the high side down or tap under the low side to raise it (**27**).

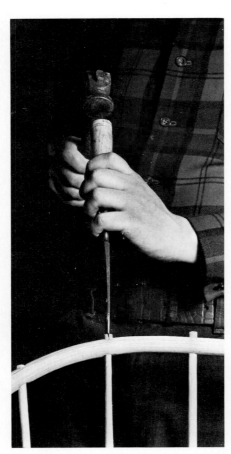

28 *When the position of the bow is satisfactory, split the ends of the spindles and wedge them into the bow.*

When you are satisfied with the position of the bow, trim the ends of the spindles and the bow with a coping saw. Leave about ¼ in. protruding from the sockets. Split the ends of the spindles with a chisel at a right angle to the grain of the bow and wedge them (**28**). Wipe glue on the wedges before driving them in. When driving the wedges, be careful not to drive too aggressively and split the bow. The change of tone should tell you when you are done, just as it did when wedging the tenons in the seat and arm.

When all seven spindles are wedged in the bow, invert the chair and wedge the ends of the bow into the arm. It is not possible to get at these from straight on, so you will have to work at a slight angle, holding the chair still on the bench with one hand (**29**).

Set the chair on the floor again and trim all the spindles flush with the bow. I shave them with a shallow gouge (**30**). Then scrape and lightly sand the end grain of the spindles and the top surface of the bow.

29 *Rest the arm on a benchtop to wedge the ends of the bow.*

30 *Shave the spindle ends flush with the bow.*

Do not shave the ends of the bow flush with the underside of the arm. The wedges will have created a slight mushroom in each end, which is thicker than the diameter of the socket. Should these joints ever loosen, the mushroomed ends will not be able to pull through the socket. The thrust of someone sitting back in the chair will tighten the joint. Although the joint will not lock, as do the leg joints in the seat, it will be tight as long as there is weight against it. If the ends pulled through, all the stress would be transmitted to the long spindles and could cause them to break.

This completes the assembly of the sack back. Clean off any spilled glue while it is still soft. You can do this by either shaving it off with a chisel, or scraping. You might want to try out the results of your chairmaking by carefully sitting in the chair. But after you do, set the chair aside so that the glue in the joints can harden. This will take a couple of hours, and by then, the chair will be ready for its finish.

Chapter IX

Assembling the Continuous Arm

The assembly of the continuous arm requires many of the same operations as the sack back. I suggest that you read Chapter VIII before starting this chapter, and that you refer back to that chapter for complete descriptions of these operations as you proceed.

First, bore the sockets for the spindles in the seat. The slope and flare angles of these spindles are indicated on the drawing at right, or you can judge the angles by eye. I start with the center socket and bore the remaining sockets in pairs, one on each side of the center. The final two sockets are those in the tailpiece for the brace spindles. These spindles are slightly flared, but have almost no slope. Beginners tend to flare the sockets too much, so I suggest that you set a bevel square to check the brace and bit while boring. Next, whittle faceted tenons on the spindles.

Spindle Angles for Continuous Arm

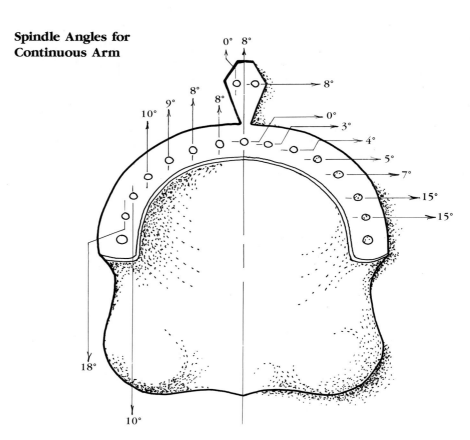

Slope is indicated on the left half of the drawing. Flare is shown on the right. Arrows indicate direction of slope or flare. The spindles are symmetrical around the center spindle.

2 To bore the armpost socket, clamp the arm and a backing board to a benchtop. Remember to start the bit perpendicular to the hand, then lower it to the proper slope and flare angles as you turn the brace. Ream the socket slowly, checking the fit with the tenon as you go.

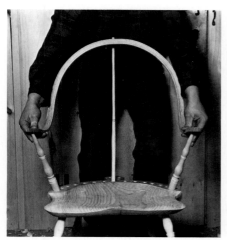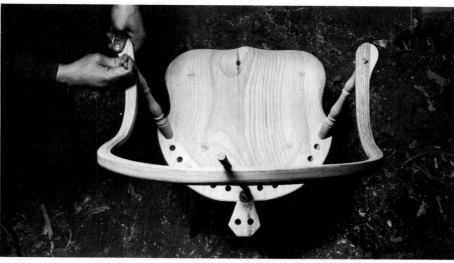

1 To locate the first armpost socket, position the arm symmetrical to the spindle sockets and mark the armpost-socket position on the hand.

3 When you sight over the arm to mark the second armpost socket, you should see something like this balanced, symmetrical relationship of arm to seat.

Socketing the arm Insert the two armposts and the center spindle in their seat sockets. Put the continuous arm in place. Rest the back of the arm against the center spindle and the hands over the armpost tenons (**1**). Sight down the arm and move it into a symmetrical relationship with the arc of the spindle sockets in the rear of the seat. Then, mark the position of the armpost socket on the top of one hand. On my chair, the socket is usually about 2¼ in. from the end of the hand. Remember to position the socket toward the outside edge of the hand to accommodate the sloping socket, but not so far that the socket penetrates the glue joint in the hand. Clamp the arm to the bench and bore the socket (**2**). I judge the angle of the brace and bit by eye; you can set bevel squares to the slope and flare angles of the armpost. Then ream the socket to fit the tapered armpost tenon.

Slip the socket onto its tenon; pivot the arm on the first socket to find the exact location of the other armpost socket. When you are satisfied with the arm's position, mark the second socket (**3**). Bore and ream this socket in the same way as the first. Place the arm on both armpost tenons and check its height. The hands should be the same distance above the seat on both sides. On my chairs, the measurement from the seat to the top surface of the hand is about 9 in. Correct any discrepancy by reaming the socket on the high side.

4 *Position the center spindle on the arm and mark its socket. Walk off the position of the two sockets on either side of the center with a pair of dividers.*

5 *Clamp the arm in a vise to bore the spindle sockets. You will have to gauge the angles by eye. The center socket, being bored here, has slope but no flare. Be sure that you do not exaggerate the slope angle.*

Insert the center spindle in its seat socket and line it up on the arm. It should slope backward, but have zero flare—it might help to use a try square to find the vertical. Mark the arm where the spindle crosses it. Then walk off the positions of the two sockets on either side of the center spindle with a pair of dividers (4). I set the dividers from a model chair; you can use the dimensions given on p. 139. At this time, you need only be concerned with the five spindles in the middle of the back.

The sockets in the arm must line up with those in the seat. It is nearly impossible to use bevel squares to check the angles, so you will have to gauge the slope and flare by eye. I bore the sockets for these spindles by placing the arm in the side vise of my workbench, held so that the hands project toward me.

Bore the socket for the center spindle first. This socket has no flare and slopes slightly, as shown in photo 5. The tendency for a beginner is to exaggerate this slope—have this fact in mind when boring the socket. To check the socket, remove the arm from the vise and insert the center spindle. (If the top end of the spindle does not slide easily into the socket, shave the end with a spokeshave until it does.) Then, put the arm onto the armpost tenons and set the center spindle's tenon into its seat socket—do not drive the tenon home. If the spindle has to be bent to reach the seat socket, put the arm back in the vise and

6 *The sockets on either side of the center socket have both slope and flare angles. Start the bit perpendicular to the arm (top), then gradually move it to the correct angles (bottom).*

7 *After boring the first five spindle sockets in the arm, dry-assemble the chair.*

adjust the spindle-socket angle in the arm by reaming it with the spoon bit. This will make the top and bottom of the socket oval, but the wedge will take care of the top, and the bottom will not be seen.

Before removing the arm, armposts and center spindle from the seat, insert the two adjacent spindles on each side of the center spindle. Line up each spindle with its mark on the top of the arm and trace its angle across the face. When you bore the sockets, aligning the brace and bit with this mark will establish the flare. Having already bored the first socket, you will have a good idea of what the slope angles for these sockets should be (6). On your first several chairs, I recommend test-fitting each spindle after its socket is bored. Eventually, you will gain the confidence to bore all the sockets at once.

When all five sockets have been bored, dry-assemble the parts. Insert the spindles in the arm, set the arm on the armpost tenons and put the spindle tenons into their seat sockets (7). Remember that these tenons are faceted so that they will bite into the soft, pine seat, so do not drive them completely into the sockets when dry-assembling. At this point, the chair begins to come together visually.

8 *Mark the positions of the sockets for the short spindles on the arm.*

9 *To bore the sockets for the short spindles, start the bit at a right angle to the arm. Establish the correct slope and flare angles by sighting along the brace and bit to the spindle socket in the seat. The clamp prevents the bit from splitting the arm.*

10 *Mark the blind sockets for the outside long spindles on the underside of the arm.*

Next, place the short spindles in their seat sockets. Mark the position of their sockets in the arm (**8**). I use the short spindles to divide the horizontal section of the arm up to the post into two equal lengths. Any difference in this spacing on either side will be lost in the transition of the bend of the arm from one plane to the other.

Bore the short-spindle sockets while the arm is on the chair. Put a *C*-clamp on the arm at the location of the socket to keep from splitting the arm while boring. Aim the bit at the corresponding socket in the seat (**9**). The arm at the locations of these sockets is thin and not rigid, so I do not put much weight behind the brace and bit. When all four short-spindle sockets are completed, lift the arm off the post tenons. Push the spindles up through the arm and drop their tenons into the seat sockets.

The next concern is the outside long spindles, two on each side. On my chairs, the arm sockets for these spindles are blind instead of through. The spindles meet the arm at such an acute angle that it would be impossible to make a neat through joint. There is also a structural reason for the blind joints. When you sit in the chair and lean back, you push the vertical section of the continuous arm backward and downward. This presses the top ends of the four blind-socketed spindles against the bottoms of their sockets. These spindles and the brace spindles limit the amount the back can flex, and they transmit the stresses to the seat.

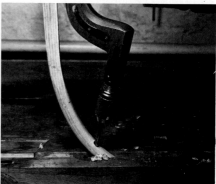

11 *Align each spindle with the mark for its socket, then draw a line along the spindle to indicate the flare angle.*

12 *The outside sockets are at an extreme angle to the arm. Raise the bit gradually to the correct angle as you deepen the hole. Check the surface of the arm with your finger, and stop boring when you can feel a dimple form from the pressure of the bit.*

Walk off the position of these sockets with dividers on the underside of the arm (**10**). Place the four spindles in their seat sockets and pinch each in turn against the arm at the mark for the socket. Trace a pencil line along each spindle to indicate its flare angle (**11**). To bore the sockets, place the arm upside down in a vise, with the hands projecting away from you. Because these sockets intersect the arm at such an extreme angle, a spoon bit is just about the only tool I know of that can do the job. Start the bit perpendicular to the arm and, as you turn the brace, raise the bit to the angle of flare indicated by the pencil line (**12**). Because of the posi-

tion of the arm in the vise, you may need to angle the top end of the brace slightly toward you. Deepen the socket until the nose of the bit begins to form a dimple on the surface of the arm. I check regularly for this dimple with a fingertip—this precaution decreases the chances of the bit breaking through.

When these blind sockets are complete, the arm and spindles are ready for assembly. (The sockets in the arm for the brace spindles, if the chair is to have them, are bored after assembly.) There is no need to make a dry-run assembly before gluing, because everything that can be tested has already been tested.

13 *Spread glue on the walls of a socket, then insert the corresponding spindle. The spindle will push glue out of the socket, but the glue remaining on the socket walls will be sufficient to make a strong joint.*

14 *Measure and adjust the height of the arm and make sure it is symmetrical to the back edge of the seat. Then trim and wedge the center spindle to fix it in place.*

Assembly I put glue into the sockets in this order: the four short-spindle sockets in the seat, the five long-spindle sockets in the center of the seat, the four short-spindle sockets in the arm, the five long-spindle sockets in the arm, the armpost sockets in the seat and, finally, the armpost sockets in the arm. (The four outside long spindles are glued and put into place later.) As you add glue to each socket in the arm, put the corresponding part into it (**13**).

When the armposts and the spindles are in the arm, insert the armposts into their sockets in the seat and coax the spindle tenons into their seat sockets. When the tenons are engaged in their sockets, tap them down with a hammer. Once in place, set the tenons with a firm hammer blow.

Measure the height of the arm at the center spindle—on my chairs, this is about 20 in. to 21 in. (**14**). Tap the arm with a hammer to adjust its height and make it symmetrical to the seat's back edge. Trim and wedge the center spindle, which will fix the arm in place, then trim and wedge the remaining spindles and the armpost tenons as described for the sack back (**15**). Shave the ends flush, then scrape and lightly sand the surface of the arm.

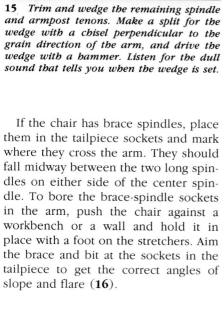

15 *Trim and wedge the remaining spindle and armpost tenons. Make a split for the wedge with a chisel perpendicular to the grain direction of the arm, and drive the wedge with a hammer. Listen for the dull sound that tells you when the wedge is set.*

16 *Bore the sockets for the brace spindles by aiming the brace and bit at the spindle sockets in the tailpiece.*

If the chair has brace spindles, place them in the tailpiece sockets and mark where they cross the arm. They should fall midway between the two long spindles on either side of the center spindle. To bore the brace-spindle sockets in the arm, push the chair against a workbench or a wall and hold it in place with a foot on the stretchers. Aim the brace and bit at the sockets in the tailpiece to get the correct angles of slope and flare (**16**).

17 *Slide the brace spindles into place after gluing the sockets.*

Put glue in the brace-spindle sockets, then slide each spindle up from underneath through its socket in the arm (**17**). Drop it down into the tailpiece socket and set it with the hammer. When both spindles are set, trim their ends above the arm, then wedge, shave, scrape and sand them.

Place the four remaining spindles in their seat sockets—the two longer ones toward the center, the two shorter outside. Pinch each against the arm where its blind socket is located and mark the maximum length of the spindle—they should butt against the bottom of the sockets (**18**). You can judge the position of the socket bottom by feeling for the dimple on the arm. The spindles may not be interchangeable, so identify each with a mark—I mark on the ends of the bottom tenons with a pencil.

Trim each spindle to the marked length and round the upper end. The round end is necessary because it will be pressed tightly into the round bottom of the socket formed by the nose of the spoon bit.

The spindles need to be steamed and bent into place. I put the spindles into my steambox, bottom tenons facing out of the box. That way, I can identify each one without having to remove it.

18 *Mark the length of the remaining spindles so they will butt against the bottoms of the blind sockets.*

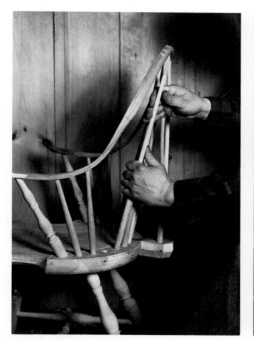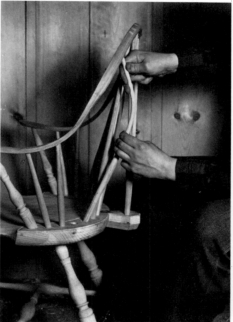

19 *Remove the pliable spindle from the steambox and quickly push the tenon into its seat socket. Space your hands apart on the shaft and bend the spindle until you can push its end into the arm socket. Straighten the spindle while it is still flexible.*

When the spindles are sufficiently pliable, decide which one to begin with and swab glue in both its seat and arm sockets. Withdraw that spindle from the box and swiftly press its bottom tenon into its seat socket (**19**). Bend it with two hands, each at a different place along the shaft. If you try to make the bend all at one point, the spindle will usually break. The bend must be distributed over as much of the shaft as possible. Once the upper end of the spindle is below the mouth of the sock-

et in the arm, slip it in and up through the socket. Straighten the spindle as best you can while it is still pliable. If a slight bow remains, you can disguise it by rotating the spindle about 45° so that the bow will then run from the front to the back of the chair and will not be seen. Follow the same procedure with the remaining three spindles.

The chair is now complete. Clean off any soft glue, and set the chair aside for a couple of hours while the glue in the joints hardens.

Finishing

All that remains to do is apply a finish to your chair. But before this can be done, the surface of the wood must be prepared. The first thing I do is wipe the saddled area of the seat with a wet sponge. This raises the grain and most of the dents or scratches in the seat. Also, glue will not absorb water, so any glue that was spilled or squeezed out of the joints will show up on the moistened seat. This glue should be scraped off, because it will not absorb a finish. When the seat is dry, I sand the saddled area with 220-grit sandpaper.

While the seat is drying, you can clean up the other parts of the chair. Scrape off excess glue; clean up any ragged edges on the bottom of the feet with sandpaper. The grain of green-wood parts will raise slightly as the parts dry, and this surface roughness can be removed by light sanding. I use 220-grit paper and stroke in the direction of the grain, not across it. I am careful not to round or soften any of the details of the turnings or remove any tool marks from the hand-worked parts. The surface will be smoothed even more when the first coat of finish is rubbed down.

The spindles that were added to the continuous-arm chair by bending need some attention. Steaming raises the grain considerably, and it can create purple stains on oak, as well as give the entire surface a slight grey cast. All of this is best removed by scraping, followed by a light sanding.

Selecting a Finish

Traditionally, Windsors were painted. This is the finish I prefer and the only one I will consent to put on a chair for a customer. But painted furniture goes against current taste. We are surrounded by plastic, chrome and other man-made materials, and the wood we use in furniture is a cherished tie to the natural world. I suspect, however, that we have come to revere the wood more than what the craftsman has done with it. When I make a chair, I put a lot of myself and my skill into it. A clear finish draws the viewer's eye to the wood, diverting it from my statement. Stain, which emphasizes the grain, is an insult added to injury. A paint finish allows the viewer to see the chair instead of the wood.

The lines of a Windsor chair are its most important visual element. The curved lines of the seat contribute to its three-dimensional, sculptured form. The legs have bold, turned outlines and are set at pronounced angles to support the chair visually as well as physically. The spindles, bent bows and bent arms are strong lines, carefully placed to achieve symmetry. A paint finish coalesces all these lines, and in addition, separates the various parts of the chair from the background.

The comment is often made that Windsors were only painted to cover the fact that so many different woods were used in the chair. On the contrary, I think the craftsmen who developed the Windsor forms had a painted surface in mind from the beginning—to a great extent, paint dictated what Windsors would look like. If a clear finish had been intended, the craftsmen would have relied on elements other than line for the chair's visual success. Instead of thin, whittled and turned parts, for example, the chair would have had broad surfaces that allow for a showy display of carefully selected woods. The joined chairs traditionally made by cabinetmakers were designed for such displays; the fine lines of a Windsor were designed to be shown off with paint.

Milk paint During the eighteenth century, when Windsors were being developed, they were finished with paint made with white lead, turpentine, linseed oil and earthen pigments. Looking at old Windsors, I have concluded that the chairmakers skimped on the lead, which was the most expensive ingredient. The resulting paint was thin-bodied, translucent and only slightly glossy. The painted surfaces were not uniform, but subtly mottled. Part of the mottle was wood peeking through the thin paint. More mottling occurred as the fugitive earthen pigments began to change color, and as the linseed oil yellowed. (Pigments that fade with exposure to light are called fugitive.) This mottled effect is very subtle—even a photograph cannot capture it. Modern glossy paints produce garish surfaces, and the matte and flat paints are too uniform and dead. I feel that a good Windsor is deserving of a finish that is at least as interesting as the chair.

I have found that milk paint produces surfaces comparable to the old paints. The origin of this ancient finish has been lost in time, but it is available today in a powdered form that requires only the addition of water. (I buy milk paint from The Old-Fashioned Milk Paint Company, Box 222, Groton, Mass. 01450.) Powdered milk paint comes in a number of colors; I am partial to the Lexington green. The manufacturer recommends mixing this green with black to get the "old-Windsor" color. I disagree, and use the Lexington green straight from the container. I also like the red, pumpkin and mustard colors; the black is dramatic, but use it with caution, for it can make a chair more visually powerful than you might want.

For those who would like to make their own milk paint, here is a formula from *The Mechanic's Own Book,* published in Portland, Maine, in 1847. (At that time, the term *mechanic* meant a craftsman or tradesman.)

Take fresh curd, and bruise the lumps on a grinding stone, or in an earthen pan or mortar, with a spatula. After this operation, put them in a pot with an equal quantity of lime, well quenched, and become thick enough to be kneaded; stir the mixture well, without adding water, and a whitish, semi-fluid mass will be obtained which may be applied with great facility like paint and which dries very rapidly. It must be employed the day it is prepared, as it will become too thick the following day. Ochre, armenian bole, and all colors which hold with lime, may be mixed with it according to the color desired; but care must be taken, that the addition of color made to the first mixture of curds and lime, contain very little water, for it will diminish the durability of the paint.

When two coats of this paint have been laid on it may be polished with a piece of woolen cloth or other proper substance, and it will become as bright as varnish. This kind of paint, besides its cheapness, possesses the advantage of admitting the coats to be laid on and polished in one day; as it dries speedily, and has no smell.

If you cannot bring yourself to paint your chairs, you will find that an oil and wax finish is easier than varnish or shellac. An oil finish can be applied by wiping, rather than with a brush. Also, it does not require rubbing down as do shellac, lacquer or varnish. Rubbing down one of these hard finishes on a Windsor is time-consuming and difficult because of all the joints and closely spaced parts.

Application Milk paint bonds best to wood that has never been finished. If the wood is left uncovered for several months, enough grime will settle on it to slow the paint's penetration. Therefore, I advise that you finish your chair as soon after completion as possible.

Mix the dry powder with water in a clean container following the manufacturer's instructions. I mix the paint in a coffee can and stir it with an egg-beater attachment in an electric drill. This method of stirring will chew up a throwaway paper bucket and might shatter a glass jar. Wait an hour or so for the froth whipped up by mixing to settle, then the paint should be water-thin. Milk paint does not keep well, so make only enough for your immediate use. You can put the paint in a refrigerator overnight, but it will not last much longer than a day or two before it spoils and loses its ability to bond.

Apply the paint with a small brush, about 1½ in. wide. Use a cheap, throwaway brush with natural bristles—avoid nylon bristles, which do not hold the water-based paint as well. Milk paint is different from other paints, so forget your experiences with oil or latex paints when you use it. It is quickly absorbed by raw wood and you cannot draw out the first coat—you almost have to daub it onto the chair.

The first coat will dry quickly—in the time it takes the water to evaporate. When it is dry, the chair will look terrible, and you will be in a state of panic, thinking that it is ruined. Do not worry. Rub down the first coat with 000 steel wool, which will polish the paint and smooth any grain raised by the water in the paint. Then dust the chair well to remove all the steel-wool fibers before applying the second coat.

The first coat seals the wood, so the second can be drawn out evenly with the brush. This coat will also dry dead flat, but there is no need to rub it down with steel wool. Because the paint is so thin, even two coats will not cover completely. Try three coats if you like, but I find that a third coat makes the surface too uniform and does not produce the effect that I like.

To complete the finish, apply a thin coat of linseed oil (be sure to buy boiled, not raw, linseed oil). Mix about four parts oil to one part turpentine. Saturate a rag with the mixture, wipe it over the entire painted surface of the chair, then wipe the oil off with a dry, absorbent rag. Do not remove all the oil, just what is standing or dripping. Set the chair aside overnight to dry; the turpentine acts as a drier, and the oil will harden enough so that you can sit on the chair the following day.

Over the next several years, the paint will undergo complex changes. The linseed oil will continue to harden, and the degree of polish that it takes will depend on the amount of friction received from hands and clothes. The resulting surface will have a whole range of textures that do not reflect light uniformly. There will be brightly polished areas, those that are less glossy, and even some that remain flat. Upon application, the yellow tint of the linseed oil will cause the paint to change color slightly; gradually, as the oil ages, it will yellow even more. Some of the pigments used in milk paint are fugitive, and will fade slightly as they are exposed to light. The yellowing oil and fading pigments will not change uniformly, giving the surface a very subtle mottle best seen when closely examined under bright sunlight. The chair still looks green, of course, but the mottled milk-paint surface is much more interesting than a single, uniform color.

As the chair is used, the paint will wear through and expose the wood wherever there is the most friction. I am very fond of this appearance; it testifies to the use and enjoyment that the chair has given to people who consider it an old friend.

Chapter XI

Sack-Back Plans

Sack-Back Windsor
Scale: ⅛ in. = 1 in.

Note: *The drawings are of a model chair. Your chair may vary from these measurements, so use them as a rough guide as you follow the instructions in the text.*

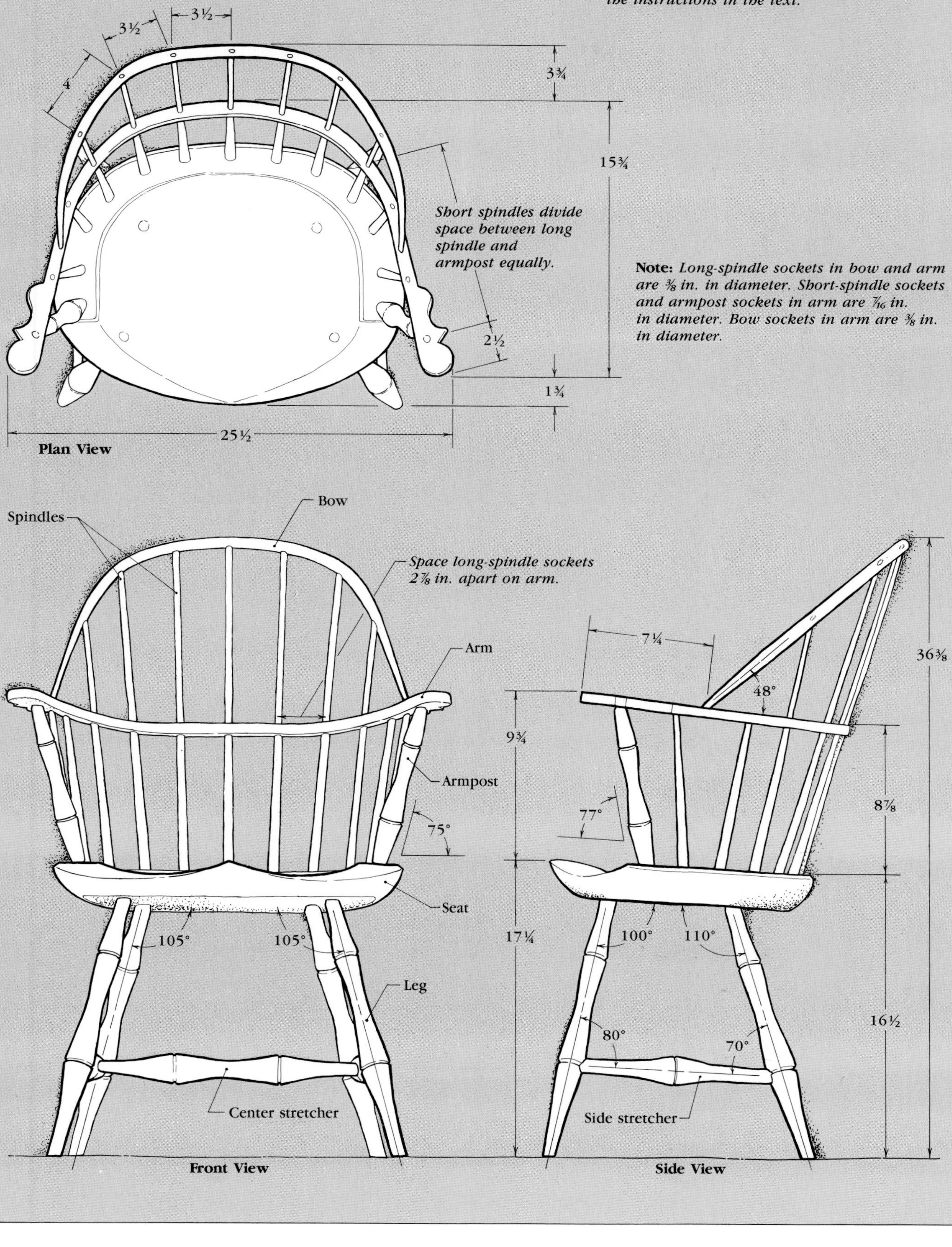

3½

3½

4

3¾

15¾

Short spindles divide space between long spindle and armpost equally.

Note: *Long-spindle sockets in bow and arm are ⅜ in. in diameter. Short-spindle sockets and armpost sockets in arm are ⁷⁄₁₆ in. in diameter. Bow sockets in arm are ⅜ in. in diameter.*

2½

1¾

25½

Plan View

Spindles

Bow

Space long-spindle sockets 2⅞ in. apart on arm.

Arm

Armpost

75°

Seat

105°   105°

Leg

9¾

17¼

7¼

48°

36⅜

77°

8⅞

100°   110°

80°   70°

16½

Center stretcher

Side stretcher

Front View

Side View

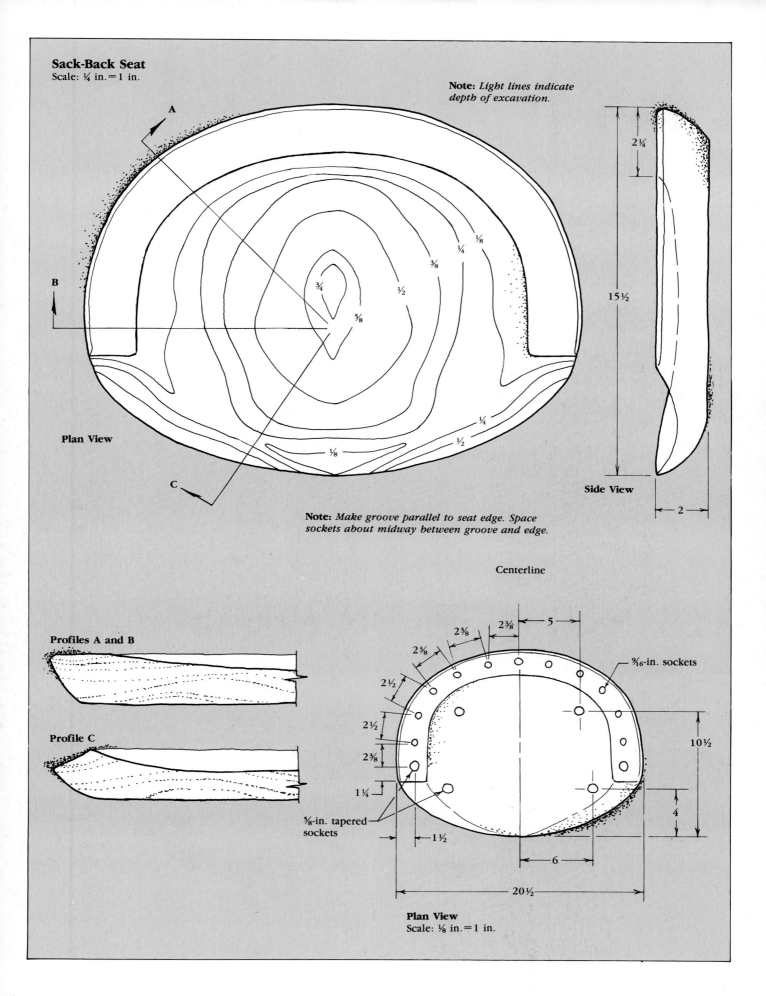

Sack-Back Seat

Scale: ¼ in. = 1 in.

Note: *Light lines indicate depth of excavation.*

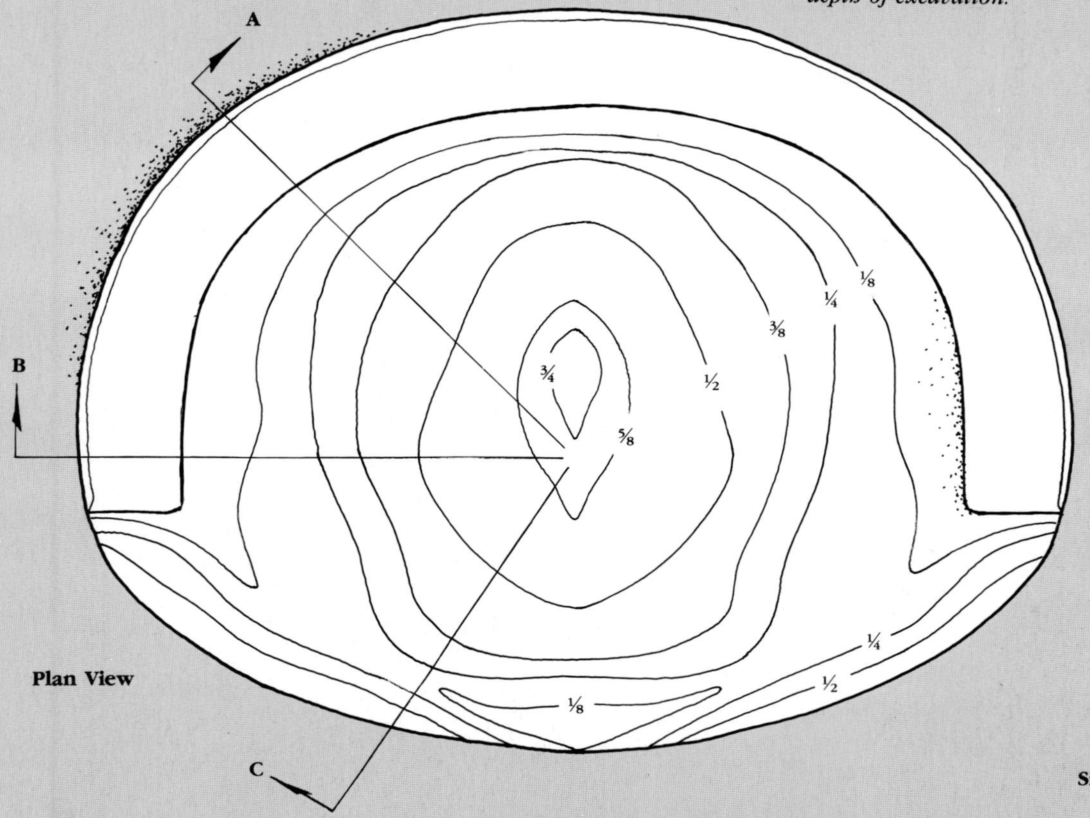
A
B
C
¾
⅝
½
⅜
¼
⅛
¼
½
⅛

Plan View

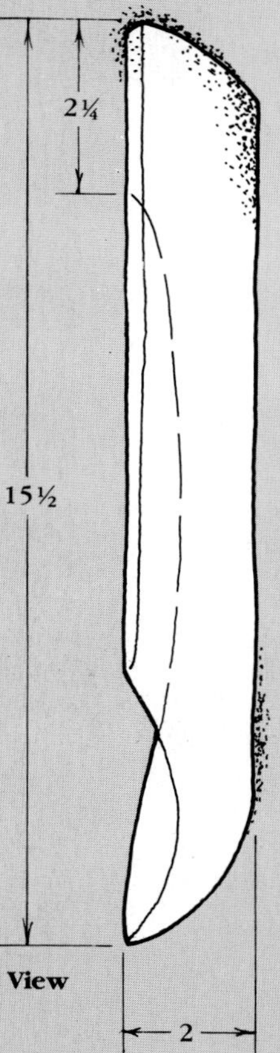
2¼
15½
2

Side View

Note: *Make groove parallel to seat edge. Space sockets about midway between groove and edge.*

Profiles A and B

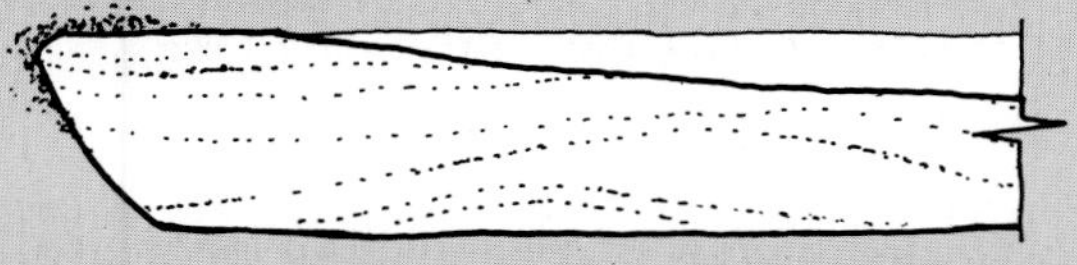

Profile C

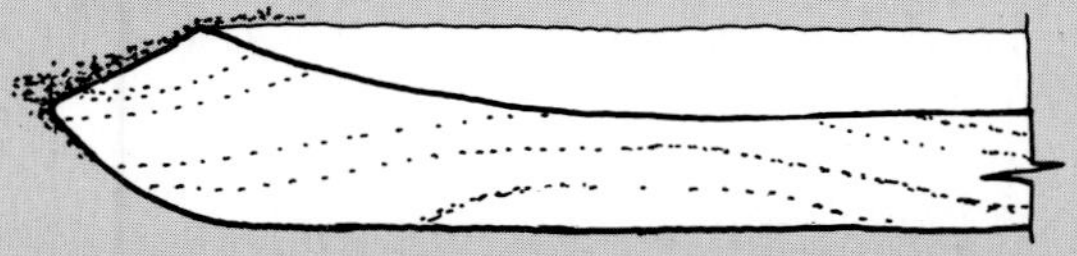

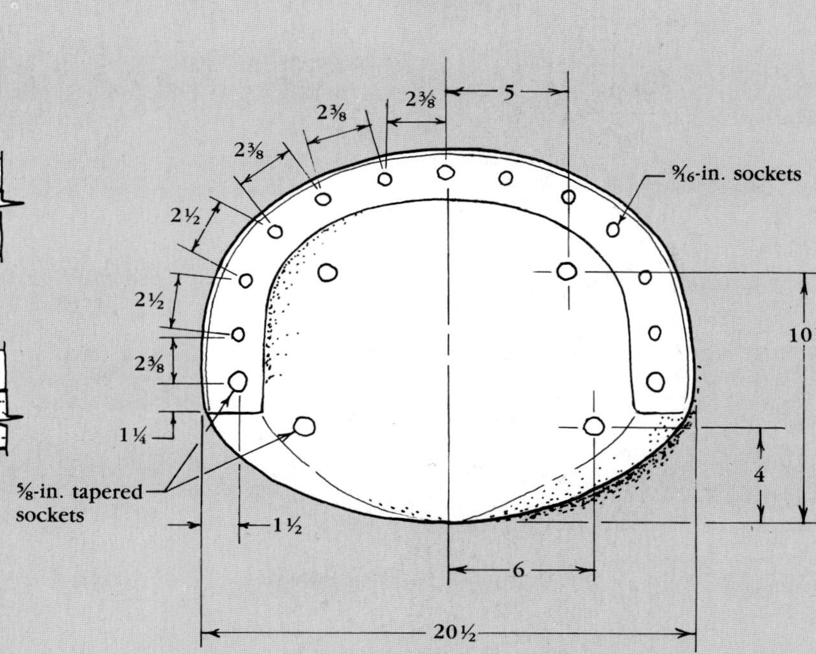
Centerline
2⅜
5
2⅜
2⅜
2½
9⁄16-in. sockets
2½
10½
2⅜
1¼
4
⅝-in. tapered sockets
1½
6
20½

Plan View

Scale: ⅛ in. = 1 in.

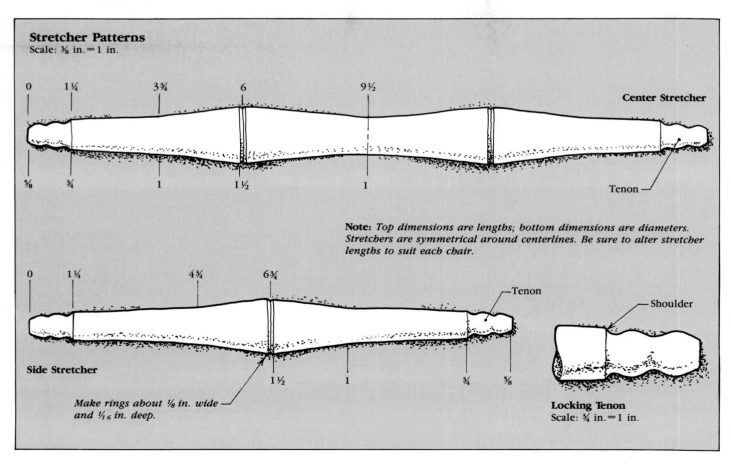

Stretcher Patterns
Scale: ⅜ in. = 1 in.

0   1¼   3¾   6   9½   **Center Stretcher**

⅝   ¾   1   1½   1   Tenon

Note: *Top dimensions are lengths; bottom dimensions are diameters. Stretchers are symmetrical around centerlines. Be sure to alter stretcher lengths to suit each chair.*

0   1¼   4¾   6¾   Tenon   Shoulder

Side Stretcher

            1½   1   ¾   ⅝

Make rings about ⅛ in. wide and 1/16 in. deep.

Locking Tenon
Scale: ¾ in. = 1 in.

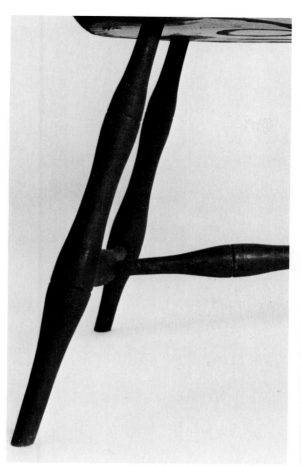

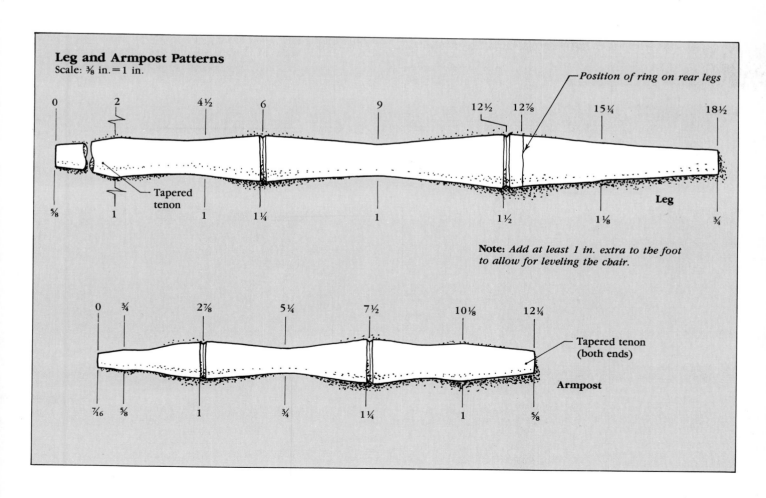

Leg and Armpost Patterns
Scale: ⅜ in.=1 in.

Position of ring on rear legs

| 0 | 2 | 4½ | 6 | 9 | 12½ | 12⅞ | 15¼ | 18½ |

Tapered tenon

| ⅝ | 1 | 1 | 1¼ | 1 | 1½ | 1⅛ | ¾ |

Leg

Note: *Add at least 1 in. extra to the foot to allow for leveling the chair.*

| 0 | ¾ | 2⅞ | 5¼ | 7½ | 10⅛ | 12¼ |

Tapered tenon (both ends)

| ⁷⁄₁₆ | ⅝ | 1 | ¾ | 1¼ | 1 | ⅝ |

Armpost

Arm, Bow and Spindle Patterns

Scale: ⅜ in. = 1 in.

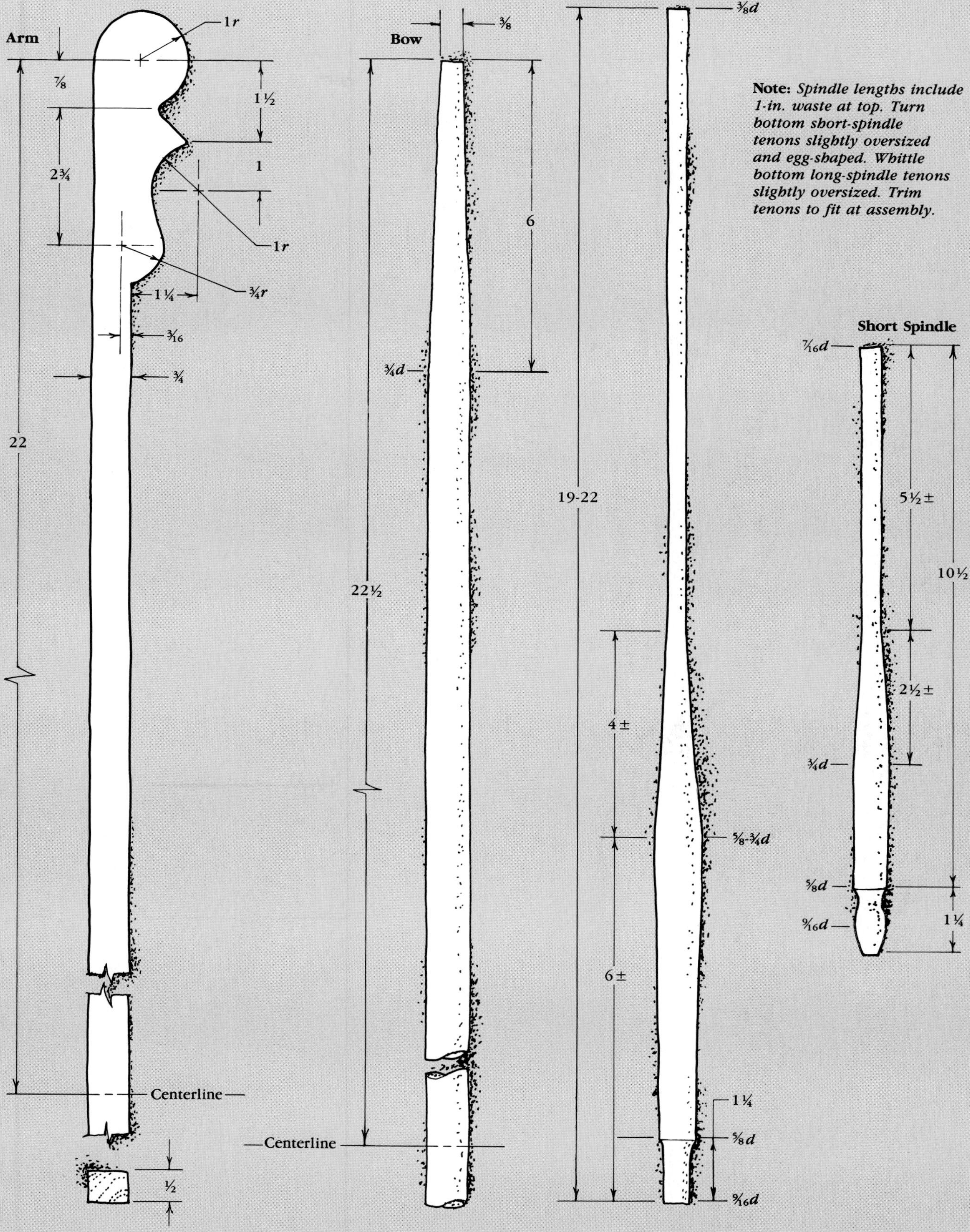

Arm
1r
⅞
1½
1
2¾
1r
¾r
1¼
³⁄₁₆
¾
22
Centerline
½
Bow
⅜
6
¾d
22½
Centerline
Long Spindle
⅜d
19-22
4±
⅝-¾d
6±
1¼
⅝d
⁹⁄₁₆d
Short Spindle
⁷⁄₁₆d
5½±
10½
2½±
¾d
⅝d
⁹⁄₁₆d
1¼

Note: *Spindle lengths include 1-in. waste at top. Turn bottom short-spindle tenons slightly oversized and egg-shaped. Whittle bottom long-spindle tenons slightly oversized. Trim tenons to fit at assembly.*

Chapter XII

Continuous-Arm Plans

Continuous-Arm Windsor
Scale: ⅛ in. = 1 in.

Note: *The drawings are of a model chair. Your chair may vary from these measurements, so use them as a rough guide as you follow the instructions in the text.*

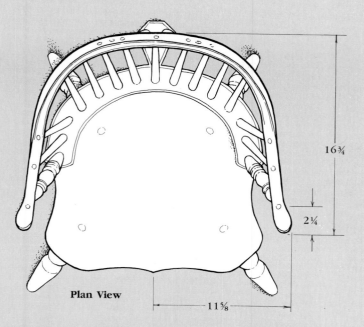

Plan View

16¾

2¼

11⅝

Note: *Long-spindle sockets in arm are ⅜ in. in diameter and 2½ in. on center, except outside long-spindle sockets, which are 3¼ in. from nearest long-spindle socket. Short-spindle sockets and armpost sockets in arm are 7/16 in. in diameter*

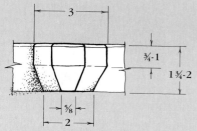

3

¾-1

1¾-2

⅝

2

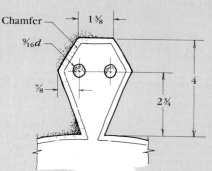

Chamfer

1⅜

9/16 d

⅞

4

2¾

Tailpiece for Brace Spindles
Scale: ¼ in. = 1 in.

Note: *Short spindles divide space between bend in arm and armpost into two equal spaces.*

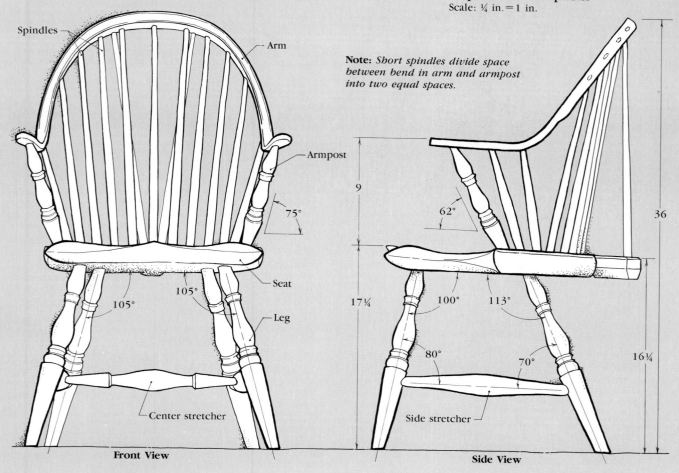

Spindles

Arm

Armpost

75°

Seat

Leg

105°

105°

105°

Center stretcher

Front View

9

17¼

62°

100°   113°

80°   70°

Side stretcher

36

16¼

Side View

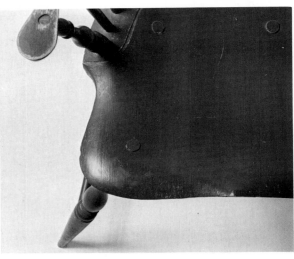

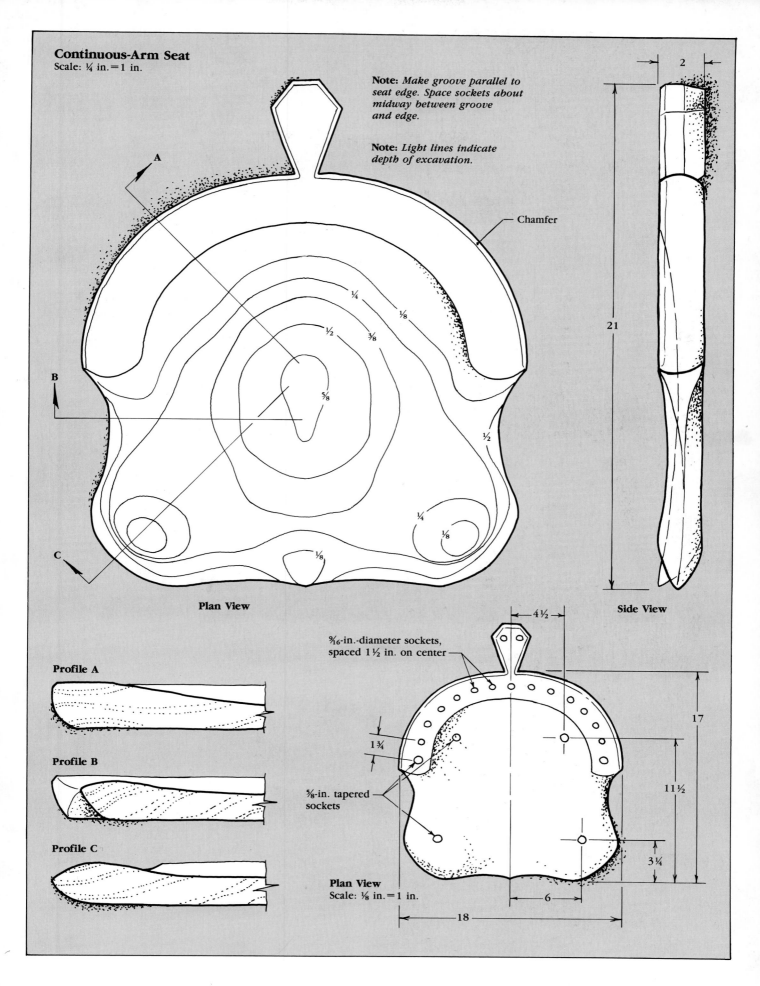

Continuous-Arm Seat

Scale: ¼ in. = 1 in.

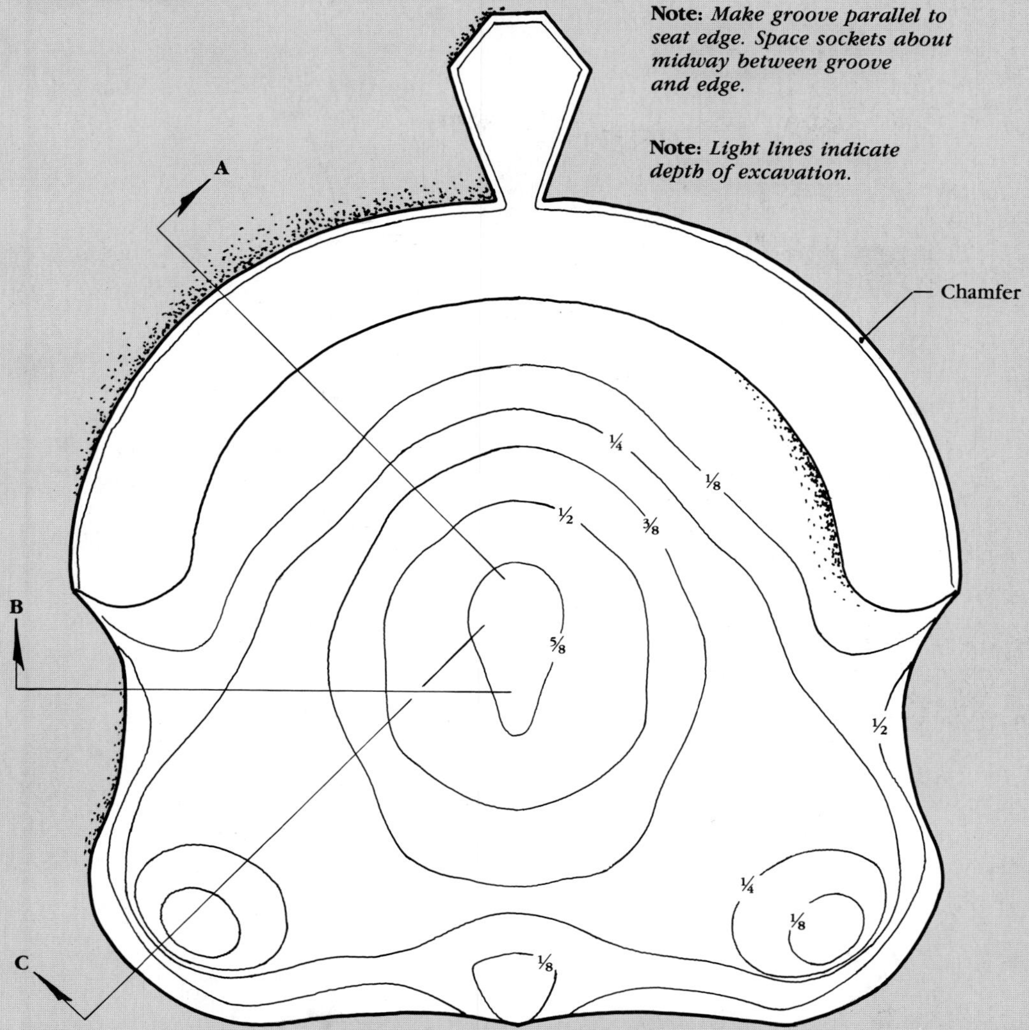
Note: Make groove parallel to seat edge. Space sockets about midway between groove and edge.
Note: Light lines indicate depth of excavation.
A
B
C
Chamfer
¼
⅛
½
⅜
⅝
½
¼
⅛
⅛

Plan View

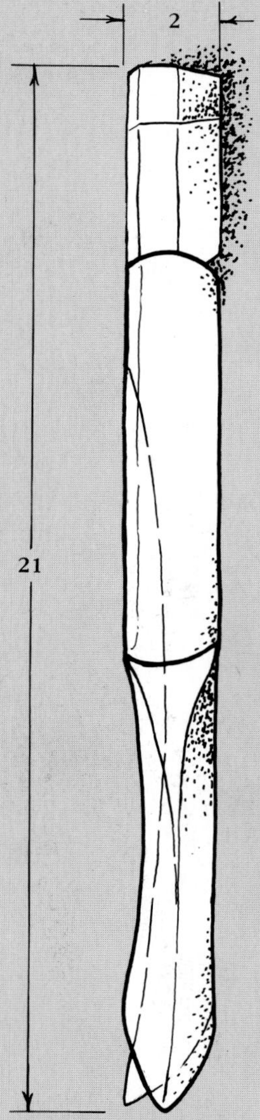
2
21

Side View

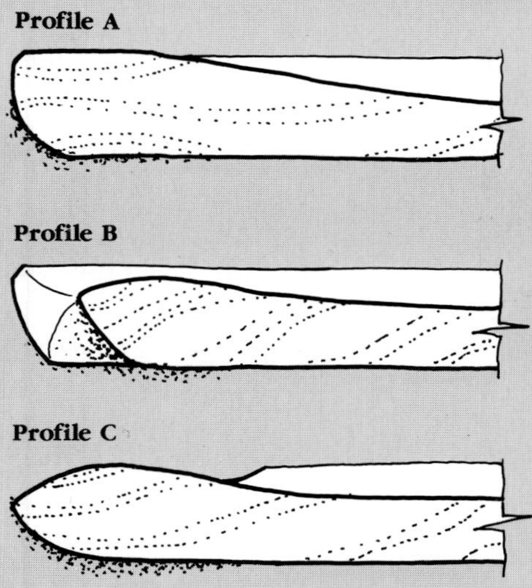
Profile A
Profile B
Profile C

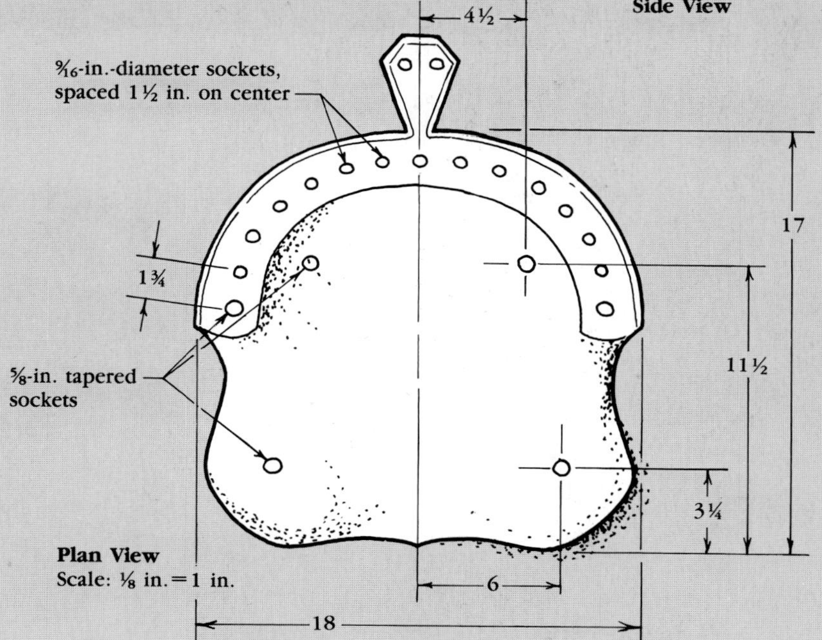
4½
⁹⁄₁₆-in.-diameter sockets, spaced 1½ in. on center
1¾
⅝-in. tapered sockets
17
11½
3¼
6
18

Plan View
Scale: ⅛ in. = 1 in.

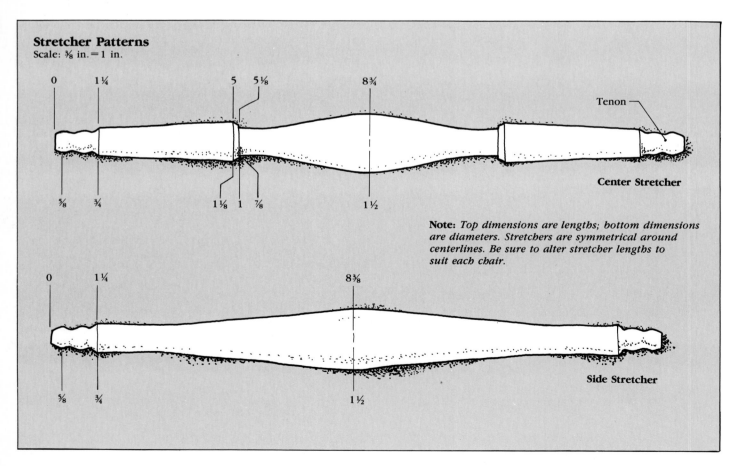

Stretcher Patterns
Scale: ⅜ in. = 1 in.

Tenon

Center Stretcher

Note: *Top dimensions are lengths; bottom dimensions are diameters. Stretchers are symmetrical around centerlines. Be sure to alter stretcher lengths to suit each chair.*

Side Stretcher

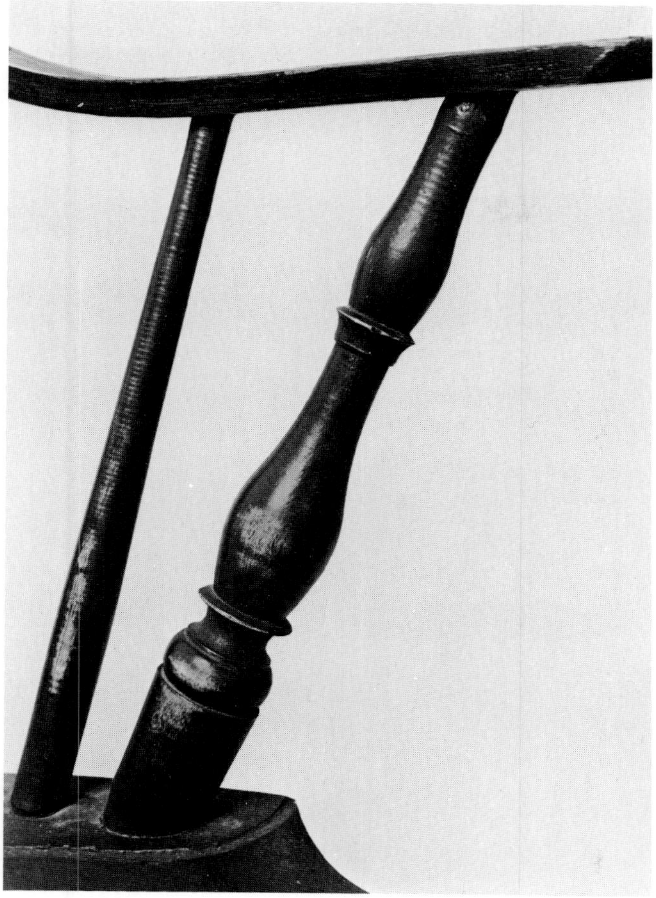

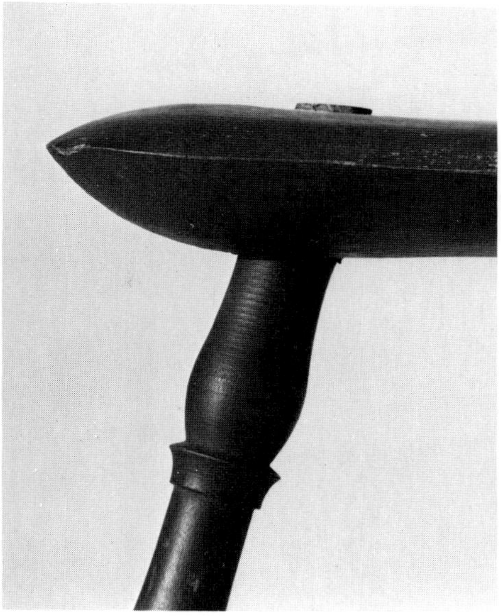

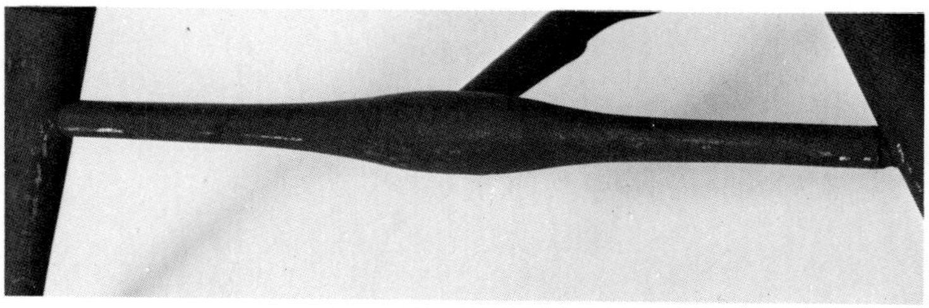

Leg and Armpost Patterns
Scale: ⅜ in. = 1 in.

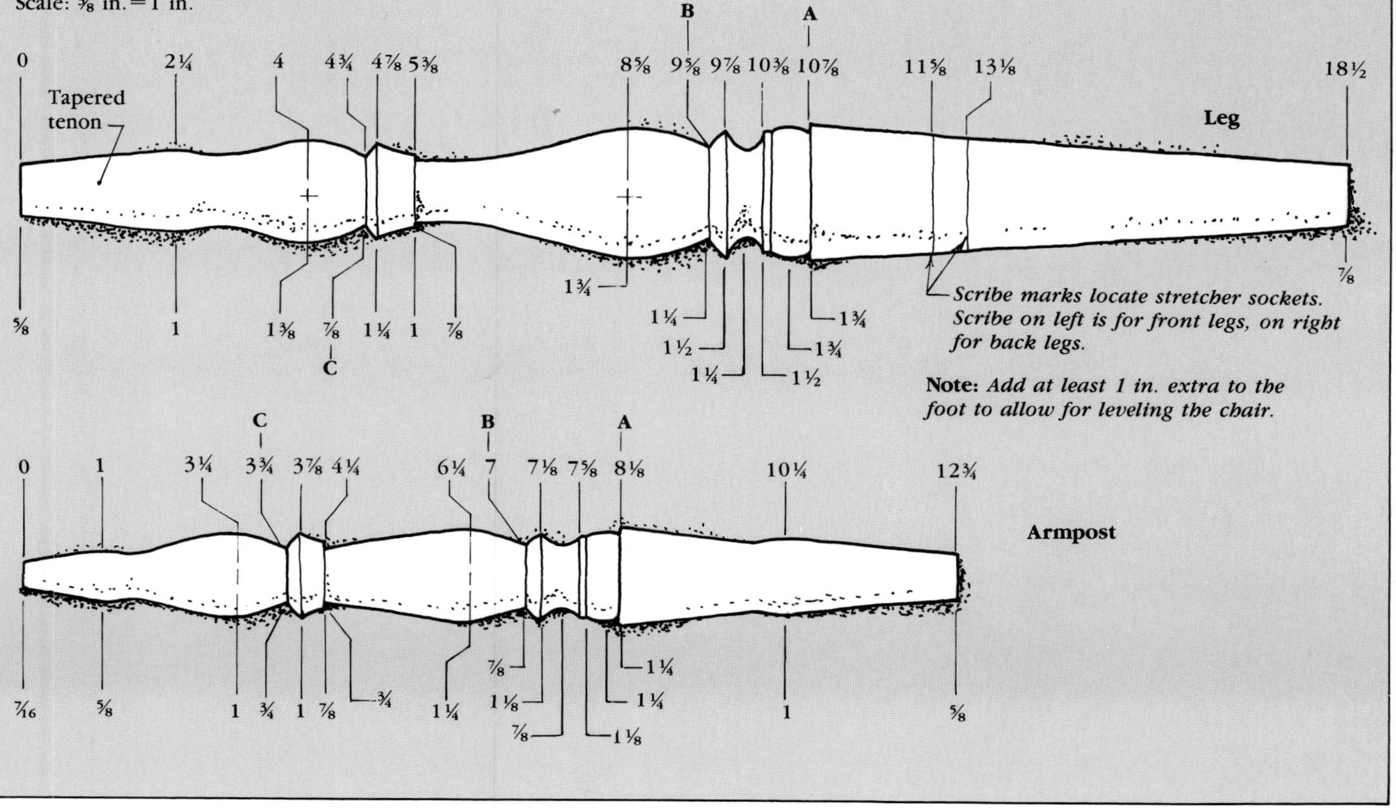

B
A
0
2¼
4
4¾
4⅞
5⅜
8⅝
9⅝
9⅞
10⅜
10⅞
11⅝
13⅛
18½
Tapered tenon
Leg
⅝
1
1⅜
⅞
C
1¼
1
⅞
1¾
1¼
1½
1¼
1¾
1¾
1½
⅞
Scribe marks locate stretcher sockets. Scribe on left is for front legs, on right for back legs.
Note: Add at least 1 in. extra to the foot to allow for leveling the chair.
C
B
A
0
1
3¼
3¾
3⅞
4¼
6¼
7
7⅛
7⅝
8⅛
10¼
12¾
Armpost
7/16
⅝
1
¾
1
⅞
¾
1¼
⅞
1⅛
⅞
1¼
1¼
1⅛
1
⅝

Arm and Spindle Patterns
Scale: ⅜ in. = 1 in.

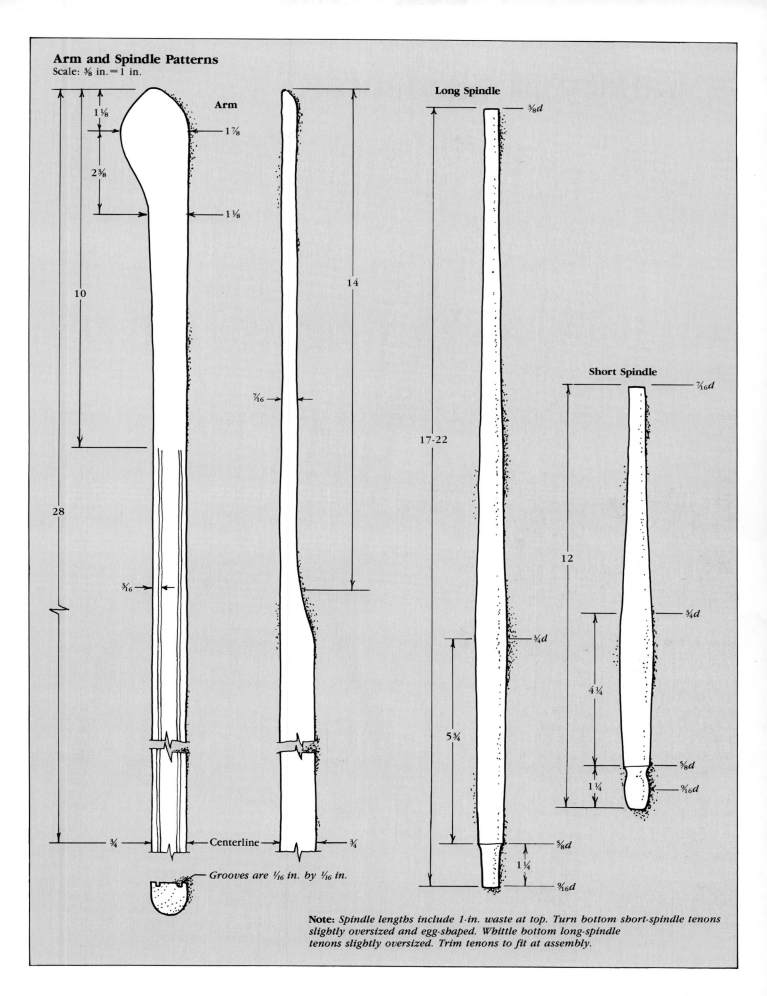

Arm

1⅛

1⅞

2⅜

1⅛

10

28

¾

Centerline

¾

7/16

3/16

Grooves are 1/16 in. by 1/16 in.

14

Long Spindle

⅜d

17-22

¾d

5¾

⅝d

1¼

9/16d

Short Spindle

7/16d

12

¾d

4¼

⅝d

1¼

9/16d

Note: *Spindle lengths include 1-in. waste at top. Turn bottom short-spindle tenons slightly oversized and egg-shaped. Whittle bottom long-spindle tenons slightly oversized. Trim tenons to fit at assembly.*

A Gallery of Windsors

1 This rod-back side chair is the first Windsor I ever owned and the one responsible for my interest in these chairs. Not long after I purchased it, I discovered that it was signed in pencil by its maker, Samuel Stickney. He worked and lived in Beverly, Massachusetts and probably made this chair about 1805. There is nothing superfluous about this chair. It is as basic as a Windsor, or any other piece of furniture, can be. It has always been painted black, a color that intensifies its starkness. The lack of elaborate detail makes it difficult to focus on any particular feature. As a result, the chair works on an almost emotional level. Someday, I would like to make a set of copies to see what effect a group of these chairs would have.

1

2

3

4

2 The legs of this fan-back side chair indicate that it was made in southeastern New England shortly after the American Revolution. The seat hints that its maker was not formally trained. It is a little too chunky, and its outline is not as refined as are the shield-shaped seats of the continuous arm and the oval back. The crest indicates that the maker was influenced by contemporary Chippendale chairs. The two turned stiles that frame the back are much more substantial than the spindles. These stiles are anchored to the seat with wedged and tapered, through socket joints that allow the back to look delicate without being fragile.

3 This chair was made during the first years of the nineteenth century, during the transition from early Windsors to Sheraton Windsor designs (see photo 5, p. 148). It retains the double-bobbin and H-stretcher undercarriage and the fully developed shield seat of the earlier chairs. The square back framed by two turned stiles, however, became typical of all Sheraton Windsors, though the stiles on this chair are not flattened as were those on later chairs. The crest rail is mortised into the stiles. Although the chair is now painted green, the original finish was red with yellow striping on the turned rings in the undercarriage and stiles.

4 Because of its distinctive back, this side chair is called a bird-cage Windsor. It is number nineteen of a set of eighteen that I was commissioned to make for Monticello, Thomas Jefferson's home near Charlottesville, Virginia. The chairs sit in the main entry to the house, replacing similar chairs that disappeared long ago and are only known through Jefferson's personal records.

In order to recreate the chairs, I worked from a sketch Jefferson himself had drawn. The top horizontal spindle is joined to the two posts of the chair back with a typical through socket joint, then carved to look like a miter. To accentuate the bold lines, the chairs were finished with black milk paint. I made this extra chair so that I could keep one for myself.

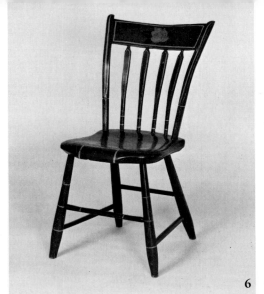

6

5

7

5 During the early nineteenth century, Windsors were still painted so that color would unify all the elements of the chair. At that time, however, the chairmaker was working in concert with the decorative painter, who was perhaps even more important to the chair's success than the chairmaker. Windsor chairmakers began to evolve designs that allowed the decorator sufficient space to add painted interpretations of the neoclassical designs and string inlay that were being used in formal furniture of the Hepplewhite and Sheraton styles. As a result, these chairs are often known as Sheraton Windsors. This chair is also called a step-down Windsor, because of the shape of its crest rail.

6 A contemporary of the step down, this arrow-back Windsor is also a decorated chair. Like the step down, it has a box-stretcher system and legs turned to resemble bamboo. (Many people mistakenly call the double-bobbin a bamboo turning—this is the true bamboo leg.) This type of undercarriage became popular about 1815 and lasted as long as Windsors were made in workshops by trained chairmakers. The vogue for decorated surfaces resulted even in flattened spindles to accommodate the decorator. Also, the shapes of the seats became more amorphous, perhaps because the bold curves that had been popular earlier conflicted with the decorated surface.

7 This arrow-back Windsor settee was probably made in Pennsylvania or Ohio during the 1830s. The settee is painted black, although it is a style that should be decorated. Most Windsor settees are basically armchairs stretched to whatever length the customer requests. The only limitation is the length of the seat material that is available. Extra sets of legs are required for strength, and are placed to divide the space beneath the seat evenly. Three heavy uprights that mimic the shape of the stiles are socketed in the seat and the bottom of the crest rail to strengthen the back. These uprights also break up the back in a manner that suggests individual places for sitters.

8 When I am assembling chairs, I find it comfortable sometimes to sit higher than the seat and other times to sit lower. I made these two stools for such use in my shop; one is 19 in. high, the other 15 in. high. The round seats are turned. The low stool was painted with a coat of mustard milk paint, then sponge-grained with a light-brown oil paint. The tall stool was painted with a coat of white milk paint, then the rings on the bobbins were picked out in green. The stylized sprigs on the legs are done in red, green and black oil paint, and the same three colors were used to create a tortoiseshell mottle on the seat.

9 I make this oval-back chair as my production-model side chair. Like the continuous arm, it can be made with or without the tailpiece and brace spindles. I offer this chair in sets, with my sack back or continuous arm as the mates. I finished the one shown in the

photograph with boiled linseed oil sealed with paste wax to show my customers how such a finish would look. In a couple of years, this finish will age to a good imitation of the old shellac finish often found on antique Windsors that were refinished forty years ago.

10 I acquired this sack-back chair long after I had worked out my own sack-back design. It was probably made by a formally trained chairmaker working in southeastern New England during the last quarter of the eighteenth century. As a chairmaker, I find the chair intriguing. The maker placed the arm 10½ in. above the seat, leaving only 10 in. between the arm and the top of the bow. This is the reverse of how I space my sack-back arm. The arm on this chair props up the sitter's elbows, rather than allowing them to hang at a natural height. This is not uncomfortable, and the chair still works visually.

11 For four years, I was the chairmaker at Strawbery Banke, a historic-restoration project near Portsmouth's city center. Peter Happny, one of the country's finest art blacksmiths, worked there at the same time, and he made the bracket for my shop sign. He included a hook at the bottom and suggested I hang a chair from it, so I made a small sack-back chair by cutting every dimension of the full-size chair in half. Some small problems with tenon and spindle thickness had to be worked out, but the result was a chair like these, just big enough for a child under five years old. The sack back proved to be so popular that I began to make a small high back as well. I still have to regulate how many of these I will make a year or I would do nothing else.

A Gallery of Windsors **149**

12

12 The double bend of the continuous arm is a shape that I have always liked to play with. This love seat is one of the results. The arm is made up of two separate pieces that are lap-joined at the location of the center post. The love seat works very well, placing the person sitting on the other side right where you want.

I finished the chair in mustard milk paint, but picked out the arm and the curved, unsaddled area of the seat beneath the arm in green. The grain of the seat runs from side to side, instead of from front to back as is usual with a shield seat.

13 This chair was the inspiration for my continuous-arm Windsor. I do not make exact duplicates of this chair, because its distinctive wedge-shaped seat would be difficult to reproduce. The seat was riven from a log, and as a result it tapers in thickness from 2 in. at the back to about 1 in. at the front. The seat appears to be just a wafer of wood, which, combines effectively with the overall delicacy of the chair.

The chair was made about 1790, probably in New York City. That it is still in service proves that it is not fragile. Its existence, and the existence of hundreds of thousands of other Windsors that have survived since the eighteenth century, are witness to the strength of these chairs.

14 A formally trained chairmaker made this oval-back Windsor, which is contemporary with the continuous arm. The results of his training can be seen in the seat, which is as refined as that of the continuous arm. Its edges are drawn so fine that they read as a line rather than as a surface. This seat strongly influenced the way I make the seats for my continuous-arm chairs.

15 Dr. Dorothy Vaughan is a good friend who has helped me considerably over the years with my research. She is a historian and does a lot of her work at the Portsmouth Athenaeum, sitting at a high clerk's desk. Dorothy developed a backache because her desk stool was too high, so my wife, Carol, suggested that I make a chair to suit Dorothy and the desk. I made the chair without telling Dorothy, and since it was near Christmas, left it at the Athenaeum, tied with a red bow, for her to discover.

From the seat up, the chair is my production-model oval back, without the braces. The double-bobbin legs are not splayed any more than those of a normal side chair, but they form a wider base because they are so much longer.

16

17

16 Known as a high-back Windsor, this chair is made only as an armchair, because without the arm, the spindles would be too weak to support a sitter. Working out this design was easy: From the arm down, it is the sack-back chair made in this book. The spindles are 27 in. long and the crest, which is steamed and bent using a clamped form, is 28 in. long. Despite the apparent fragility of the spindles above the arm, they are strong and supple because they are made of riven wood.

17 I used the continuous-arm back to make this daybed. I placed the center stretchers so that they run front to back, rather than side to side. By so doing, I avoided the problem of arranging the side stretchers in straight lines on either side of the undercarriage. The spindles that connect the crest to the seat are each a single shaft.

I padded and upholstered the seat so that it can be used comfortably for long periods of time. A pillow can be suspended from the crest to support the

sitter's head in a position suitable for reading. The daybed is finished with black milk paint, and its red upholstery is outlined with brass-headed tacks.

18

18 This fan-back armchair is my own personal chair. I wanted a comfortable place to relax at night, and this design allowed me to make a large chair with good proportions. The chair is 44 in. to the top of the crest, and the seat is 17 in. deep by 24 in. wide, big enough for a cushion, two dogs and me. The crest is steamed and bent using a form and clamps. The chair has three coats of milk paint: the first green, the second red and the third black. This produces an interesting effect as the chair wears.

Chapter XIV

Sharpening Chairmaking Tools

A number of the chairmaking tools used in this book may not be familiar to most woodworkers. I have already discussed how to use these tools, and here will explain how to sharpen them. I will assume that you are familiar with the basic techniques of grinding and honing common woodworking tools, such as chisels and planes. If you are not familiar with these techniques, you can find them explained in most introductory woodworking books.

The tools I use for sharpening are quite simple and unsophisticated. They are also readily available and inexpensive. Like nearly every other woodworker, I own a bench grinder. I still use the same machine I bought secondhand some thirteen years ago for six dollars. It still has one of the original wheels on it; I never replaced it because I never use it. I purchased the 5-in., medium-grit wheel that I do use at about the same time as the grinder itself. At the rate I am using it, that wheel will last longer than the electric motor. Long ago, I removed the tool rests from the grinder because I prefer to grind free-hand and found that the rests were only in the way.

I maintain the grinding wheel with a diamond dresser. This is nothing more than a piece of round steel stock, about the size and length of a cigarette, with an industrial diamond set in the center of one end. Diamond dressers are much faster and more effective than are any other grinding-wheel dressing tool that I have used. They are inexpensive and can be purchased from machine-shop supply houses.

The dresser is used to keep the wheel from wearing out of round, which would cause it to wobble (**1**). The tool also strips away particles of steel clogging the wheel's surface. A clogged wheel requires more pressure to shape a cutting edge. This pressure increases the friction between tool and wheel, which creates more heat—too much heat and you risk burning the steel and losing the temper.

Hold the dresser at an angle to the axis of the wheel and just touching the wheel's edge. Move the diamond across the surface in a steady motion, so that it clears a smooth surface rather than one that is corrugated. (Always wear a face protector when using the dresser.)

1 *Use a diamond dresser to true the edge of a grinding wheel.*

2 *You can make a buffing wheel from an electric motor and buffing pads impregnated with abrasive compound (shown in foreground). The wheel is a big help in obtaining a razor-sharp cutting edge quickly.*

3 *Oilstones for sharpening chairmaking tools are, from left: a soft-Arkansas-grade stone, a hard-Arkansas-grade stone, an India gouge slipstone, and a square, soft-Arkansas-grade slipstone. The cylindrical stone is also soft-Arkansas grade, and is useful for honing tools with curved cutting edges.*

The only other machine I use in sharpening is a buffer. Buffing replaces the old method of stropping a cutting edge on a piece of leather to create the final, razor-sharp edge. When possible, I also use the buffer to remove the small, steel burr that is created on the edge by grinding. This method is less time-consuming than honing on oilstones to remove the burr. When buffing, hold the tool very lightly against the pad, usually for a very short time, and be careful not to round over the cutting edge.

I made my own buffer from an old washing-machine motor, which I attached to a wide, 2-in.-thick, pine baseboard and wired to a standard box and switch, like those used for light switches in a house (**2**). The motor is fitted with a split arbor and two 5-in.-diameter buffing pads. Arbors and pads can be purchased at most hardware stores. I snipped the stitching of the pads about 1 in. back from the circumference with a razor blade to make a 2-in.-wide, fluffy buffing surface. Impregnate this surface with grey-steel abrasive compound by holding a block of compound against the pads as they spin.

The remainder of my sharpening equipment consists of several oilstones, an India gouge slipstone and several files (**3**). I am not exactly sure what my oilstones are made of, because I either purchased them secondhand or inherited them. One stone, for example, is amber in color and cuts like a hard Arkansas. It belonged at one time to my great-great-uncle Billy, who was a pattern maker after the Civil War. It descended from him to my grandfather, then to my father, then to me. Anyway, it is what I use to get a final edge. To sharpen all the tools mentioned in this chapter, you will need only two Arkansas oilstones, one hard and one soft, each about 1 in. by 2 in. by 6 in.; a 1-in.-square by 5-in. or 6-in.-long, soft Arkansas slipstone; and an India gouge slip.

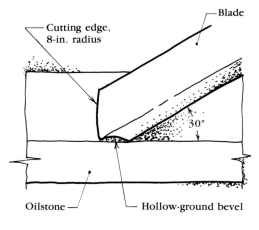

4 *Hone the entire length of the radiused cutting edge of a foreplane blade.*

Foreplane If you surface a lot of rough-sawn lumber by hand, a foreplane with a convex cutting edge will make your work a lot easier. I grind the cutting edge of my foreplane blade to about an 8-in. radius along its length, and an angle of about 30°. The grinding wheel produces a hollow-ground bevel, which is easier and quicker to sharpen than a flat bevel.

After grinding, hone first on a soft Arkansas stone (4). Because the cutting edge has been ground to a radius, it is difficult to hone it in the familiar figure-eight pattern. I work the edge either back and forth or with a circular motion. While I do this, I slowly move the cutting edge through its arc, so that the entire curve is honed. If the edge has a burr after this honing, I remove it by holding the blade lightly against the buffing wheel. Next, hone on a hard Arkansas stone, and gently remove any trace of a burr on the buffer.

Honing a Foreplane Blade

Cutting edge, 8-in. radius

Blade

30°

Oilstone

Hollow-ground bevel

As the cutting edge begins to dull, you can hone it again on the hard Arkansas stone. This is possible because of the hollow-ground bevel; to hone the entire width of a flat bevel, you would have to begin with a coarser stone. I can sharpen many times by honing before I have to regrind the bevel. This is why I have been able to live for so long with my old, beat-up grinding wheel—I do not use it very often.

I shape the blade of my small compass plane to a 3-in. radius. It is sharpened in the same way as the foreplane blade. The compass-plane blade is made of an old file and is much harder than bench-plane blade. Because I only use it on pine seats, it has to be honed as seldom as twice a year. I cannot recall having to regrind the bevel more than two or three times in all the years that I have owned and used that plane.

5 *Hone the concave curve of a forkstaff-plane blade with an India gouge slip.*

6 *Hold the drawknife in a vise and work the stone over the bevel in a circular motion.*

Forkstaff plane The cutting edge of the forkstaff-plane blade is concave, rather than convex. This shape conforms to the curve of the plane's sole. On my plane, this is a 3-in. radius. I have never had to regrind this blade. I use it only to round sack-back bows and one surface of the continuous arm, so it does not need to be kept as sharp as a bench plane. About twice a year, I hone the edge with the India gouge slip and light buffing (**5**).

To hone, hold the blade in a vise so that the bevel is facing you, and work an India gouge slip in a circular motion on the bevel. As you do this, move the stone across the entire length of the curved edge. If you need to grind the blade, it might help to work the edge of the grinding wheel to a radius with the diamond dresser. Alternatively, you can shape the edge with a half-round file, which can remove a lot of metal quickly; a chainsaw file also works in a pinch.

Drawknife I keep my drawknife up to snuff with a stone that is the equivalent of a soft Arkansas. I hold the blade of the drawknife in my tin-knocker's vise, gripping it near one of the handles, and work the stone over the bevel in a circular motion (**6**). This is a much less awkward method than moving the knife over the stone. Be careful to hone the entire length and width of the bevel, so that the cutting edge does not gradually become rounded. Use the same motion on the underside of the blade to turn the burr over. I hold the stone flat on the underside, and do not form a second bevel. A drawknife maintained in this way should never need grinding. As much as I use mine, I sharpen it in this manner only several times a year.

8 *Use a file to reestablish the bevel of a spokeshave iron.*

7 *Use a flat oilstone to hone the bevel on the outside of the scorp and a round slip or an India gouge slip to turn the burr that forms on the inside of the curve.*

Scorp A scorp's cutting edge is maintained in the same manner as a drawknife's. Hold the scorp in a vise near one of its handles and move the stone over the blade. My scorp is bent to a 2⅛-in. radius, so I use a soft-Arkansas-grade stone about 1 in. square and 6 in. long to work the bevel on the outside of the curve (**7**). The India gouge slip can be used on the inside surface of the blade to turn the burr. Move both stones in a circular motion. It is difficult to grind one of these tools on a bench grinder, but if you buy a new scorp, the bevel can be quickly established with a file. After filing, you will have to rely on patient work with a coarse oilstone, using the same method as for honing.

Spokeshaves My spokeshaves receive a lot of use, and their cutting edges need to be maintained regularly. The spokeshave that I use for whittling spindles eventually develops a hollow in its cutting edge, and this has to be removed. The blade is too small to hold on a grinding wheel, and removing the hollow by honing would take too long. I use a file instead. Because the edge is so short, I prefer a triangular file. Grip the blade near one end in a vise, and hold the other tang with your free hand to prevent vibration (**8**).

9 *Hone a spokeshave blade with a square, soft Arkansas stone. Work the bevel, then turn the burr with the stone flat on the blade.*

10 *Use an India gouge slip to hone the inside surface of a travisher blade.*

Once the file has reestablished the bevel and straightened the cutting edge, hone the blade with a square, soft Arkansas stone (**9**). If a heavy burr develops, remove it by buffing, then return to honing with the stone. Finally, strop the cutting edge lightly on the buffing wheel.

Travisher This tool is similar to the spokeshave and is sharpened in the same manner. The square Arkansas stone will not work on the beveled inside curve of the blade, therefore, I use the India gouge slip on this surface (**10**). My travisher is never used on wood other than pine, and even then its only function is to produce a finished surface. Consequently, its cutting edge does not require the same regular care as a spokeshave.

11 *Work the nose of a spoon bit to a perfect radius on an India gouge slip.*

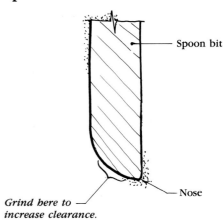

12 *Buff the shaped spoon bit inside and out to finish the cutting edge.*

Spoon bits When sharpening new spoon bits, the first step is to make the curve of the nose symmetrical. Once that is done, the bit can be honed; otherwise, very little work is required to keep the edge sharp. I establish the curve of the nose with an India gouge slip. Set the bit right up on its nose, very nearly perpendicular to the surface of the stone (**11**). Then work the nose to a radius by pivoting it from side to side on the slip. When the nose is shaped, buff it inside and out (**12**). You can push the nose into the buffing wheel fairly hard—I use more pressure for a spoon bit than for any other tool.

Test the edge of the bit by mounting it in a brace and pushing the nose into a piece of hardwood. Be sure that the edge is at a right angle to the direction of the grain. The nose should pierce the wood easily, and as you turn the brace, the typical spiral chip should result (**13**). If it merely produces powder, the bit is scraping and is either insufficiently sharp, or lacks sufficient clearance. If it lacks clearance, grind away a bit of the metal behind the cutting edge, as shown in the drawing at right.

Spoon-Bit Clearance

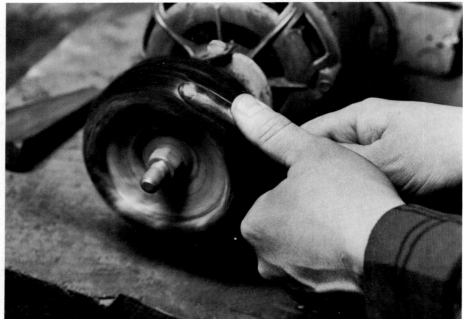

Spoon bit

Grind here to —
increase clearance.

Nose

13 *A sharp spoon bit should cut quickly and produce a crisp, spiral chip.*

14 *Sharpen a reamer by filing its edges flat, then honing with a medium-grit stone.*

A properly sharpened spoon bit will cut in a very aggressive manner. After every half-dozen or so sockets, I restore the edge by buffing the inside and outside of the nose for several seconds. Every month or so, I hone the nose for a very short time on the India slip. Never grind the cutting edge of a spoon bit. The edges of the bit's body above the nose never require attention.

Tapered reamer The reamer is a companion to the spoon bits. It makes a scraping cut, and when it is sharp, a reamer will produce shavings rather than just dust. To sharpen a reamer, hold it in a vise by its tang and run a file along the two upturned edges, then hone with a medium-grit stone (14). Be careful to file the edges flat; when the arrises become rounded, the tool will not cut cleanly and will need touching up with the file and stone.

Cross Section of Reamer

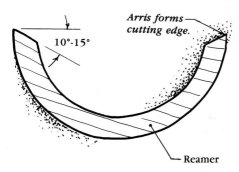

10°-15°

Arris forms cutting edge.

Reamer

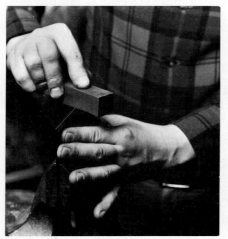

15 *Flatten the scraper's edge and remove the old burr with a file (top right and left). Then hone the edge and faces with an oilstone. Be sure not to round the edge.*

16 *A wheel burnisher makes fast work of creating a scraper burr. Push the burnisher hard against the scraper's edge.*

Cabinet scraper I use a cabinet scraper for finish work—smoothing and cleaning up parts that have already been shaped. A small burr of steel running the length of the scraper's edge does the cutting; a sharp scraper will raise a nice curl of wood rather than dust. To prepare the scraper for this burr, hold it in a vise. First, file the edge flat; I use a file held in a saw-sharpening jointer to do this (**15**). This tool ensures that the edge of the scraper is square to its faces. File the faces to remove any of the remaining old burr; keep the file flat on the faces.

Cross Section of Cabinet Scraper

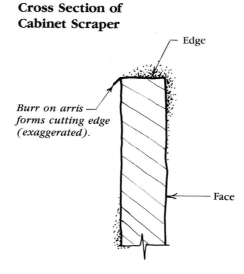

— Edge

Burr on arris forms cutting edge (exaggerated).

— Face

Next, hone the edge and faces with a soft Arkansas oilstone—be sure not to round the edge. Honing removes the rough marks of the file and makes for a stronger, more uniform burr. I turn the burr with a wheel burnisher, a tool specially designed for this purpose (**16**). I hold the scraper in my vise and place the burnisher so that its wheel contacts the edge. I then bear down with as much pressure as my arms will supply and pull the burnisher over the edge in a single, smooth pass. One pass creates a perfect burr. I find this method is fast and foolproof. When the scraper produces dust, not shavings, it is time to file, hone and turn another burr.

17 *Sharpen a gutter adze by honing the cutting edge with an India gouge slip and buffing, inside and out.*

Gutter adze The gutter adze also has a curved cutting edge. Because I use it only once a week to chop out two pine chair seats, I can maintain the edge by just honing with the India gouge slip, and then buffing lightly. Grip the adze in a vise to hold it steady while honing (**17**). Work the slip over the entire length and width of the bevel in a circular motion. (This will remove most nicks; a chainsaw file will take care of heavy nicks.) Remove the burr on the buffer. If you make your own adze, you can create the bevel with a half-round file. I have never had to do anything but hone my adze, and I expect to be able to say the same when I am an old man.

Splitting hatchet I use my Kent hatchet only for riving, so it requires no care. You can remove nicks in the cutting edge with a file, but they will not prevent it from wedging a billet of wood apart. If you want to use your hatchet for cutting as well as for splitting, sharpen the cutting edge as you would that of a regular ax.

Froe I use a froe as a lever for splitting and do not drive it into the wood, so it should also last forever without sharpening. If you drive a froe to start a split, you may want to sharpen its cutting edge with a file. But remember that a froe should split rather than cut. A sharp cutting edge could cut the wood fibers rather than wedge them apart.

Bow saw I do not think that sharpening bow-saw blades is worth the effort—long before a blade needs filing, it breaks from metal fatigue. Store-bought replacement blades are expensive, so I make my own from ¼-in., six-point bandsaw blades.

Index